EXCEL MADE EASY

(3 in 1) A Visual Step-by-Step, Fully Illustrated Crash Course to Master Excel Fast; Boost Efficiency and Productivity with Practical Examples, Custom Formulas, and Expert Tips

Gavin George

TABLE OF CONTENTS

BOOK 1: FUNDAMENTALS OF EXCEL MASTERY

INTRODUCTION

Welcome to the world of Excel, a tool so powerful and versatile that it has become indispensable in modern workplaces. My name is Gavin George, and I'm here to guide you on a journey from novice to expert, transforming how you view and use Excel.

Imagine sitting at your desk, faced with an overwhelming amount of data. Now, consider the satisfaction of efficiently organizing that data, discerning patterns, and making data-driven decisions swiftly. This is the potential Excel holds for you, and this book is your map to unlocking that potential.

"Excel Made Easy" is structured to help you step confidently through the basics into more sophisticated uses of Excel. In this first part, the "Fundamentals of Excel Mastery," we begin at the beginning. Here, you'll learn not just to walk but to run with Excel as your reliable partner. You'll start by understanding why Excel is so pivotal in most jobs today. We'll explore the interface that might seem daunting at first but will soon become as familiar as the back of your hand.

Next, we dive into the nuts and bolts with creating and managing workbooks. I'll show you, with vivid illustrations, how to save, retrieve, and share your Excel files—a fundamental skill in collaborative environments. From there, we will master the art of manipulating rows and columns and step into the world of effective data presentation and organization.

With each example, I aim to equip you with not only the how-tos but also the why-dos. We will troubleshoot common problems together, and I'll share tips and tricks to enhance productivity and efficiency, ensuring that you don't just perform tasks but understand the logic behind them.

As we progress, every formula you write and every data set you manage will build your confidence. By the end of this book, not only will Excel be demystified, but you will also be on your way to becoming the office Excel guru. Ready to get started? Let's dive in and turn the seeming complexity of Excel into your tool for success.

THE SIGNIFICANCE OF EXCEL IN MODERN WORKPLACES

In the vast sea of digital tools and software that flood the modern workplace, Microsoft Excel stands out—not just as a program for inputting data, but as a comprehensive tool that transforms raw data into valuable insights. This section explores the pivotal role that Excel plays in various sectors and how it can catapult your career to new heights, making it an indispensable skill in your professional toolkit.

Consider the global reach of Excel: it's used in virtually every industry, from healthcare, where it manages patient data and schedules, to finance, where it performs complex financial modeling and risk analysis. Its versatility is unmatched, providing both novices and seasoned professionals with the tools needed to interpret and visualize data effectively. Whether you're managing small projects or large-scale databases, Excel gives you the power to handle tasks efficiently and with precision.

Think about a typical day at any modern office. Marketing teams analyze consumer data to forecast trends, finance departments track and report on budgetary allocations, and human resources manage everything from payroll to employee performance metrics—all using Excel. This utility makes it more than just software; it's a critical thinking partner that helps businesses make informed decisions, strategize, and maintain operational efficiency.

Beyond its practical applications, Excel's significance in the workplace also extends to career development. Proficiency in Excel is often a prerequisite for many roles, particularly positions that require data manipulation and analysis. Mastering Excel can lead to job security, higher earning potential, and career progression—not to mention a significant competitive advantage in the job market.

For instance, consider the role of an analyst or a data scientist. These professionals rely on Excel not only for storing and sorting data but also for performing complex statistical analysis. Excel's functions, from basic formulas to advanced macros, help them draw meaningful conclusions from raw data. Moreover, the ability to transform this data into compelling visual stories is pivotal in policymaking, strategy sessions, and stakeholder presentations. Excel's capability to pivot, graph, and translate data into digestible formats makes it a storytelling device, not just a spreadsheet tool.

Let's delve into a real-world scenario to illustrate Excel's impact. Imagine a retail company that tracks sales data. Through Excel, this company can identify the most popular products, predict sales peaks during specific times of the year, and tailor marketing strategies to boost revenue. Furthermore, by analyzing customer feedback data collected via Excel, the company can improve product offerings or address service shortcomings—actions directly linked to customer retention and satisfaction.

In education, administrators use Excel to monitor student performance, manage timetables, and even predict future resource needs through trend analysis. This ease of management and prediction underscores Excel's adaptability across different fields, showcasing its breadth and depth.

For you, the aspiring Excel wizard, understanding these applications enhances not just your job performance but also empowers you to offer solutions that can optimize workflow, reduce costs, and increase profitability. Each function you master opens up further possibilities for innovation within your role, making you a pivotal member of your team.

Moreover, Excel fosters a collaborative environment. Its compatibility with various cloud platforms allows for seamless sharing and communications. Teams can work on the same document from different locations, making remote collaborations effective. This feature is increasingly important in today's global workspace, highlighting Excel's role in not only data management but in building and maintaining dynamic team dynamics.

Now, pair this collaborative capability with Excel's evolution. Regular updates and the integration of artificial intelligence features are set to not only enhance user experience but also introduce smarter, more efficient ways to process data. This means that Excel will continue to be relevant and a critical tool in professional settings for years to come.

To gear up for this continuous evolution, part of our journey through this book will be to cultivate an advanced understanding of Excel's features — going beyond surface-level functions and diving deep into what makes Excel a powerhouse in data management and decision-making. Through detailed examples and step-by-step guides, you'll learn how to navigate Excel's rich feature set, enabling you to handle larger data sets with confidence, precision, and efficiency.

The significance of Excel in modern workplaces cannot be overstated. By mastering it, you are essentially learning the language of modern business. As we delve further into this guide, keep this perspective in mind: each skill you acquire is not just about getting better at using a tool; it's about becoming a more strategic thinker and a more valuable asset to any team.

MAXIMIZING BENEFITS FROM THIS INSTRUCTIONAL GUIDE

Embarking on the journey of mastering Excel with this guide is like setting sail on a voyage to uncharted territories where the promise of treasure (or in our case, invaluable skills) awaits. Each turn of the page will propel you forward through the fathomless depths of Excel's capabilities, ensuring that you harness the full power of this formidable tool by the end of our exploration.

To maximize the benefits from this instructional guide, consider this your navigator's map, charting a course that avoids common pitfalls and directs you towards the most efficient routes to Excel mastery. Here, we aim not only to educate you on the functions and features of Excel but also to enrich your understanding in ways that transform these technical skills into practical, workplace-enhancing abilities.

Understanding the Layout and Structure

The structure of this guide is intentionally designed to build your knowledge base from the ground up. It starts with the essential concepts and gradually moves toward more complex functionality. This tiered learning approach ensures that foundational knowledge is solid before advancing to more intricate operations. To benefit fully, I encourage you to engage with the content in sequence. Skipping ahead might be tempting, especially for those with some Excel background, but the incremental learning process ensures no critical details are missed, which could be pivotal for mastering advanced content later on.

Engaging with Step-by-Step Tutorials

Each chapter is equipped with detailed, step-by-step tutorials that are not just instructions but pathways carved to enhance your understanding. As you follow these steps, try to replicate the examples in your copy of Excel. Learning by doing not only reinforces the material but also increases your confidence in using Excel for various tasks. If anything feels unclear or you make an error, simply revisit the steps. The guide is crafted to be revisited, with each iteration helping you consolidate your understanding.

Applying Practical Tips and Real-World Scenarios

To bridge the gap between theory and practice, this guide is peppered with practical tips and real-world scenarios that align with tasks you might encounter in your daily work or personal projects. These are not just hypotheticals but drawn from actual workplace needs and challenges. Integrating these examples into your learning process will help you see the relevance of each feature and function, making the learning process engaging and practical.

Utilizing Visual Aids

Humans are visual creatures, and Excel, with its grids, charts, and data visualizations, is a highly visual tool. This guide takes full advantage of that by including high-quality images and screenshots to accompany instructions and explanations. These visuals serve as both guides and reassurances, showing you not only the steps to achieve a task but also what your screen should look like once you've done it correctly. Make sure to closely observe these images as each highlights subtle yet important details that enhance your comprehension and execution of Excel functions.

Incremental Learning and Review

Each chapter culminates with a summary that recaps essential points and sometimes introduces how these might be expanded upon in subsequent chapters. Use these summaries for review before progressing to ensure retention and comprehension. This cyclical review reinforces learning and solidifies your ability to recall and apply information as you move forward.

Embracing Errors as Learning Opportunities

Mistakes are inevitable, especially when confronting a complex tool like Excel. Rather than discouragement, view each error as a learning opportunity. Each error encountered and corrected deepens your understanding of why things work the way they do in Excel. This guide will help illuminate common mistakes and offer troubleshooting tips to rectify them, fostering a learning environment where challenges are embraced, not feared.

Interactive Learning

Lastly, to fully engage with this guide, I encourage interactive learning. This involves practicing beyond the scope of the examples provided, experimenting with functions, and applying what you learn to different data sets or hypothetical scenarios. The more you manipulate and interact with the data, the more intuitive Excel's tools and features will become.

By incorporating these approaches into your study, this guide will serve far more than just an instructional manual; it will become a springboard for innovation and efficiency in your Excel usage. Whether for professional development, academic needs, or personal projects, the skills you acquire here will enable you to leverage Excel's capabilities to their fullest, turning complex data into actionable, understandable insights that empower decision-making and drive success.

CHAPTER 1: FOUNDATIONS OF EXCEL

Welcome to the world of Excel, a tool so powerful that it can transform the way you handle data, analyze information, and present your findings. As we embark on this learning journey together in "Foundations of Excel," you're not just opening a textbook; you're unlocking a whole new realm of possibilities that can significantly enhance your workflow and productivity

Imagine you're at your workplace, and a deluge of data that looks like a tangled web lands on your desk. Your task? Make sense of it, extract valuable insights, and maybe even present it in a way that's understandable to everyone, from interns to CEOs. That's where Excel becomes your best ally.

In this chapter, we're laying down the solid groundwork needed to navigate this robust tool. We'll start with the basics—getting to know different versions of Excel. This might seem straightforward, but understanding which version you're working with is crucial as it determines the tools and features at your disposal.

Next, we'll tour the Excel User Interface. Picture this: you're a pilot in the cockpit of a plane. Just as a pilot needs to understand what every lever and button does to fly safely and efficiently, you'll need to familiarize yourself with where everything is located in Excel and what each function is responsible for. Knowing how to efficiently find and use the features you need will save you time and spare you unnecessary frustration.

Following that, we're moving into how to effectively manage and organize your workbooks. This is akin to knowing how to file your documents in the right cabinets and drawers in a large office. Whether it's creating a new workbook or finding the best ways to save and share your documents, mastering these skills means ensuring that your data isn't just well-organized but also secure and easily accessible to those who need it.

Every step of the way, I'll provide you with practical, real-world examples to illuminate the abstract parts of this tool. For instance, when we look into how to create and manage workbooks, I'll show you exactly how each function can be applied to streamline tasks in an actual business setting.

By the end of this chapter, you will have all the foundational skills at your fingertips, allowing you to navigate Excel's interface with confidence and use its basic functionality to organize and manage data efficiently. Let's dive in and start transforming that intimidating data into powerful insights.

COMPREHENSIVE OVERVIEW OF EXCEL VERSIONS

Embarking on a journey with Excel, akin to embarking on a historical exploration, is both exhilarating and enlightening. As we lay out the historical tapestry of Excel versions, it's not merely about the chronology but understanding how each iteration has expanded the horizons of what's possible with data. Starting with Excel's inception and moving through to its latest incarnation, we'll uncover how these evolutionary steps can be leveraged to enhance your daily tasks and decision-making processes.

With the debut of Microsoft Excel in the mid-1980s, originally designed for the Apple Macintosh, a new era in digital computing emerged.

Excel was one of the first software to utilize a graphical interface effectively, allowing users to interact with their electronic sheets visually. This was a monumental leap from its predecessors, which relied heavily on textual commands.

As we moved into the early 90s, Excel began to dominate PCs with its Windows version. This version introduced features that many today can't imagine Excel without, such as toolbars and the ability to format cells with colors. Imagine being one of the first users, delighting in turning a plain grid into a colorful report with just a few clicks—a small step in functionality, a giant leap in data presentation.

Fast forwarding to the early 2000s, Excel 2003 showcased the introduction of list commands and XML data, tools that allowed users to manage complex data more efficiently. Reflect on the first time you could pull data from the web directly into your spreadsheet. It wasn't just about seeing the data; it was about interacting with it dynamically and extracting more nuanced insights.

With the arrival of Excel 2007, the world was introduced to the Ribbon interface, an innovation aiming to make features more accessible compared to the multitude of nested menus in prior versions. The introduction of more sophisticated data visualization tools such as color scales and icon sets in conditional formatting allowed even a novice to articulate compelling data stories visually. Think of it as moving from pencil sketches to vibrant watercolor paintings—a transformation in how data could be visually interpreted and presented.

This trend of enhancement continued with Excel 2010, which introduced Sparklines, miniature charts that fit in a single cell. Now, consider how summarizing trends within a data set right beside the data points could optimize your analysis process, allowing for quicker decisions in a fast-paced business environment.

Excel 2013 brought a significant stride forward with the introduction of Flash Fill and Quick Analysis tools, further simplifying the mundane tasks of data organization. Imagine the relief when what once took several tedious steps to format and extract data could now be accomplished with a single click or drag of the mouse.

Progressing to Excel 2016, users witnessed the integration of more powerful analytical features like Power Query and Power Pivot, fundamentally enhancing the robustness of Excel's data modeling capabilities. Envision the possibilities as you effortlessly merge tables from various sources, conducting complex data analysis that once required specialized software.

Excel 2019 refined these features and introduced new functions like TEXTJOIN, CONCAT, IFS, and more, continuing to simplify complex tasks with more intuitive solutions. Each function is like adding a new tool to your toolbox, making what once seemed a complex task now seemingly effortless.

As we embrace Excel for Microsoft 365, a continuously updated version, the boundaries of collaborative and cloud-based functionalities are being pushed. Real-time collaboration, AI-powered insights, and automation streamline workflows in unprecedented ways. Data is no longer just a solitary spreadsheet but a dynamic, interactive canvas of insights and opportunities.

Understanding the historical context and capabilities of each Excel version isn't merely academic—it's a practical exploration of how you can apply these evolutions to your contemporary tasks. Each version built upon the last, adding layers of functionality and simplicity, guiding you through a logical progression in mastering this powerful tool.

As you familiarize yourself with these versions, consider your specific needs. Are you primarily conducting deep data analysis? Are you leveraging Excel's vast visualization tools to make data-driven stories compelling? Or perhaps, you're optimizing the collaborative features to manage projects across teams? Your focus will dictate which features from which versions will serve you best, much like choosing the right type of fuel for your car to ensure optimal performance.

By now, grasping the sequential development of Excel should feel less like a technical rundown and more like fitting pieces of a puzzle—each version offers unique tools and features, fitting into your workflow puzzle based on your specific tasks and goals. This journey through Excel's history is not just about witnessing growth; it's about equipping you with the knowledge to harness each version's potential fully, ensuring your Excel proficiency is not just current but cutting-edge.

NAVIGATING THE EXCEL USER INTERFACE

Imagine stepping into a complex control room with buttons, switches, and screens. It's a little overwhelming at first, right? That's often how many of us feel when we first open Microsoft Excel. But don't worry; it's about to make a lot more sense as we navigate through the Excel User Interface together. By the end of this journey, what seemed like a panel of perplexing buttons will transform into familiar tools that empower you to handle your data with ease.

The Excel Environment

When you launch Excel, you're greeted by what we refer to as the 'Ribbon'—a central element in the Excel interface. This is not just a static part of the user interface; it's your gateway to Excel's diverse functionalities. The Ribbon is organized into tabs, such as Home, Insert, and View, each housing a group of related tools. Think of it as a well-organized toolbox where every tool is grouped by function—the hammer and nails are together, so to speak.

Navigating the Ribbon is your first step in mastering Excel. The Home tab, for example, is where you'll find the fundamental tools for formatting text and numbers, adjusting cell styles, and managing cells. When you're creating reports or organizing data, these tools are indispensable, allowing you to highlight critical insights swiftly and make your data readable at a glance.

Working with the Quick Access Toolbar

Above the Ribbon lies the Quick Access Toolbar—a small, customizable toolbar where you can pin your most frequently used commands. This customization allows you to streamline your workflow by keeping essential tools like Save, Undo, or Redo just a click away, regardless of which tab you are in. Imagine you are painting a picture, and instead of reaching out constantly for a palette, you have your favorite colors attached right above your canvas—this is what the Quick Access Toolbar does for your data management tasks.

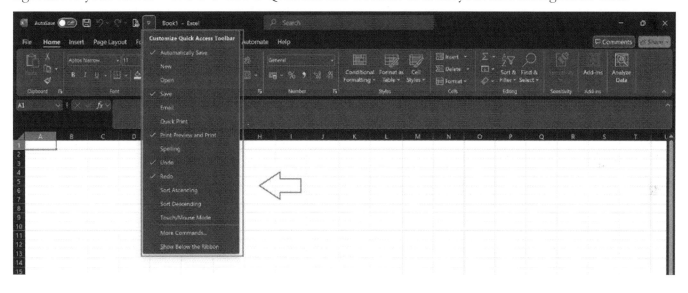

Exploring the Backstage View

The File tab, often referred to as the Backstage View, is like stepping behind the scenes of your Excel workbook. This is where all the major document management commands reside—from creating and saving files to inspecting document properties and managing accounts. If the Ribbon is the control panel, Backstage View is the management office where you ensure everything is orderly and setup as needed.

Moving through these areas in Excel might initially seem daunting. However, each section is logically organized just like chapters in a book, guiding you from starting a document to saving, protecting, and sharing it. It's navigating through a story—your story told through data.

Utilizing the Formula Bar

One cannot talk about navigating Excel without highlighting the Formula Bar. This feature displays the data or formula contained in the active cell. You can think of it as your data decoder—it converts cell addresses and numerical codes into understandable formulas or results. By mastering the Formula Bar, you not only see the raw data but also understand how the data is computed, offering insights into not just what your data is, but how it's calculated.

Handling Worksheets and Workbooks

The terms 'worksheets' and 'workbooks' might seem confusing at first. Simply put, a workbook is like the entire book, while a worksheet is akin to a page within that book. Excel allows you to navigate between multiple worksheets within a single workbook easily. This is crucial, as maintaining data in separate worksheets can help organize and manage related data effectively—a vital skill in ensuring data clarity and ease of access.

When you work with multiple worksheets, you'll use the sheet tabs located at the bottom of the Excel window to switch between them. You can also add, rename, or delete worksheets to better organize your data 'chapters'. This flexibility is key in handling complex data sets where segmentation is necessary for clarity and focus.

Handy Tips for Getting Around

Here are some practical tips to enhance your navigation skills:

- Utilize keyboard shortcuts, like 'Ctrl+S' to save your work frequently or 'Ctrl+Z' to undo any mistakes promptly. It's like having a quick reaction capability that keeps you efficient and ensures your work remains error-free.
- Make use of the 'Freeze Panes' in the View tab to keep an eye on key data or headers as you scroll through the rest of your worksheet. It's like having navigation markers in a long document, helping you not to lose sight of context.
- Regularly customize the Ribbon and Quick Access Toolbar to fit your specific workflow needs. The more personalized your tools, the easier your tasks will be.

As you continue to explore and interact with the Excel User Interface, remember each element is crafted to make your data handling smoother and more intuitive. With each click and each navigation, you'll find Excel less like a daunting control room and more like a powerful, responsive cockpit from which you can pilot your data destiny with precision and ease.

WORKBOOK CREATION AND MANAGEMENT

Creating and managing workbooks in Excel is akin to being the architect of your own detailed library. Each workbook you create can act as a comprehensive binder, where numerous worksheets hold vast amounts of data, calculations, and analyses. As we dive into understanding workbook creation and management in Excel, think of yourself as both an architect planning the structure and a librarian cataloging and safeguarding valuable information.

Starting with a New Workbook

When launching Excel, the first step is often creating a new workbook. This process sets the foundation for your data projects. Simply opening Excel will present you with the option to start a new workbook. It's as though you're opening a blank canvas, ready to paint your data story onto it. Remember, a new workbook typically opens as 'Workbook1', a default name which, like naming a newly discovered planet, should be renamed to reflect the contents it's going to hold.

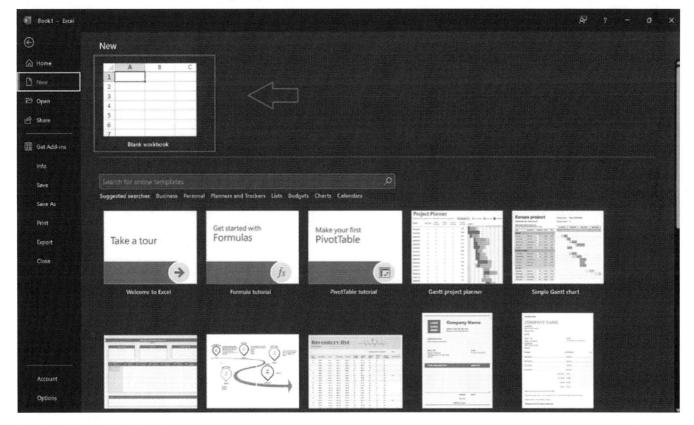

Saving Your Workbook

Saving your workbook is a fundamental practice; it's the equivalent of locking the treasure chest after adding valuables. Excel provides a plethora of saving formats, each serving different purposes and needs. The default format, .xlsx, suits most needs by allowing macros, graphics, and complex formulas to function smoothly. While saving, choosing the right folder and path is akin to selecting a secure and accessible spot on your vast bookshelf, ensuring quick access whenever needed.

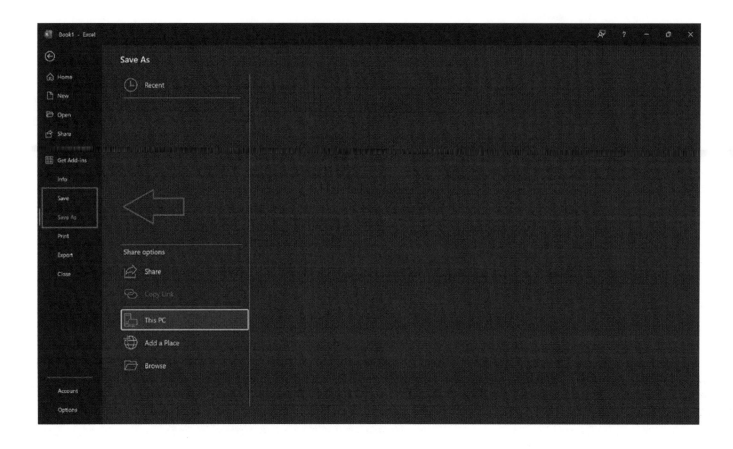

Managing Worksheets Within Workbooks

Each workbook can house numerous worksheets. Adding a new sheet is like adding a chapter to your book. It's here in these sheets that your data lives. To add a sheet, simply click the '+' icon next to the existing sheet tabs. This action is straightforward but powerful, allowing your workbook to expand in scope and detail.

Renaming a worksheet is just as important. The original names, such as 'Sheet1', 'Sheet2', etc., are like temporary placeholders. By right-clicking on a sheet tab and selecting 'Rename', you give your worksheet a meaningful name that reflects its content. This step is crucial for navigation, especially when workbooks grow to hold myriad data sets.

Organizing Worksheets

Imagine needing a specific document and knowing exactly which drawer and folder it's in. Similarly, in Excel, you can reorder your worksheets by clicking and dragging their tabs to new positions. This simple maneuver helps in maintaining a logical flow of data, akin to arranging chapters in a manner that the story unfolds naturally. If your work pertains to chronological data, organizing sheets from January through December, for instance, makes your data story logical and intuitive.

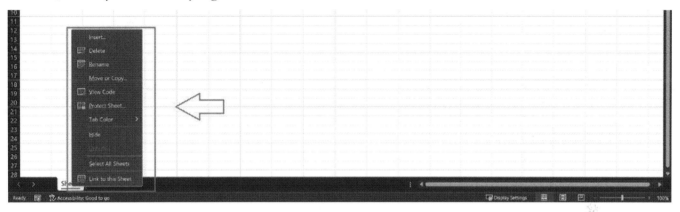

Protecting Your Data

In your digital data library, protection is key, especially when your workbook contains sensitive or critical information. Excel allows you to safeguard this by protecting the workbook with a password. This process is like closing a book with a lock and ensuring that its contents are changed or viewed only by those who hold the key. Under the 'Review' tab, selecting 'Protect Workbook' initiates this security feature, prompting you to create a secure password.

Sharing and Collaborating

Modern problems require modern solutions. In today's interconnected world, collaboration is inevitable. Excel adapts to this need beautifully with features that allow you to share your workbook. Through Excel for Microsoft 365, you can invite colleagues to view or edit a workbook, ensuring that everyone has the most updated version. This collaborative feature is akin to working on a group project where each member can contribute their expertise simultaneously.

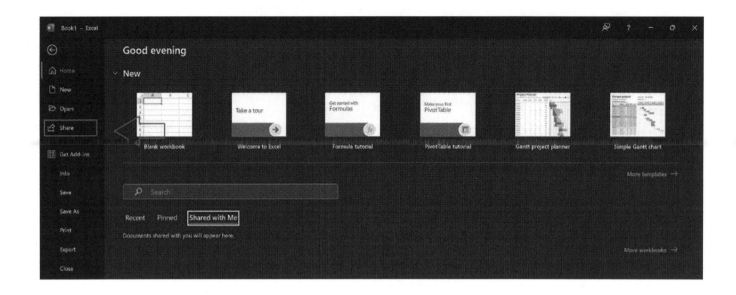

Printing Your Workbooks

Even in our digital age, the need to print documents remains, and Excel makes this easy. By configuring print settings, you can control exactly how each worksheet appears when printed. Adjustments such as setting print areas, scaling to fit, and selecting specific worksheets to print are similar to choosing which parts of a manuscript to publish. It ensures that the final print represents only the necessary and relevant data, tailored suitably for the audience or purpose.

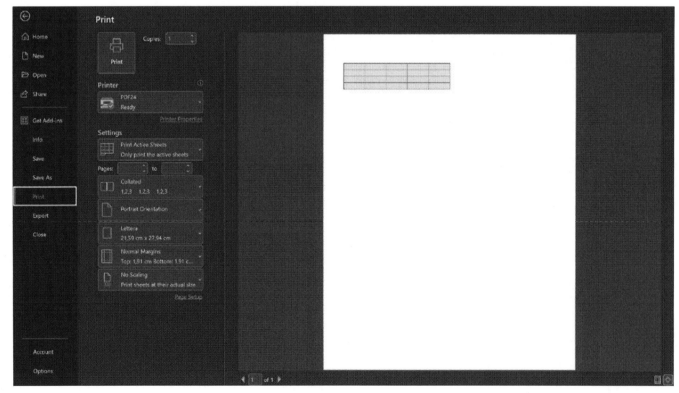

Practical Tips for Efficient Workbook Management

1. **Regularly Save Your Work**: Just as you'd save a draft of a critical email or document, frequently saving your work in Excel prevents data loss and ensures your latest inputs are secured.

2. **Utilize Color Coding**: Just as a librarian might use different colored labels for different genres, coloring tab names of related sheets or important cells can make navigation quicker and reduce errors.

3. **Create a Master Document**: If your work involves multiple related projects, consider creating a master workbook that links to others. This way, you have a central hub from which all related data can be accessed, like a main directory or index.

In essence, mastering workbook creation and management sets you on a path to becoming proficient in Excel. It's about building confidently on the foundational blocks of data entry to complex analysis, transforming raw data into actionable insights. Each workbook is not just a file; it's a chapter in your ongoing story of data exploration and utilization.

TECHNIQUES FOR SAVING AND SHARING DOCUMENTS

In our journey through Excel, understanding how to save and share your documents is akin to mastering the art of preserving and distributing literature. It's essential, whether you're working solo or collaborating across a team. This segment dives into the nuanced techniques of safeguarding your data through saving and sharing, embodying practices that cater to both security and efficiency.

Saving Essentials

Saving your worksheet in Excel is more than just pressing Ctrl+S; it's about knowing the various formats available and choosing the right one for your needs. Each format serves a distinct purpose, impacting how your data can be viewed and used by others.

Choosing the Right File Format

The default format for saving Excel files is .xlsx, which supports most features without restrictions. However, other formats like .xls for older Excel versions or .csv for simple, comma-separated files, cater to specific needs. For instance, saving a file in .csv format strips away all formatting to sheer values, ideal for systems that require raw text input.

AutoRecover Feature

The AutoRecover feature in Excel is like an insurance policy for your data. It saves a copy of your workbook at regular intervals to prevent data loss during unexpected shutdowns. To make the most out of this feature, ensure it's enabled via File > Options > Save, and set your preferred save interval. Think of it as a backup generator that kicks in to protect your work, giving you peace of mind.

Advanced Saving Options

Password Protection

When dealing with sensitive data, securing your document with a password ensures that only authorized personnel can access it. This can be done when saving your file—simply choose File > Save As, find the Tools button next to the Save button, select General Options, and set your password. It's akin to locking a diary; it becomes a private repository, assessable only by those who hold the key.

Document Properties

Adding properties to your documents—such as titles, tags, and comments—can be invaluable for organization and searchability. This metadata acts like an index card in a library catalog, making it easier to retrieve amidst vast collections of data files.

Sharing and Collaboration Techniques

In an era of teamwork and collaborative efforts, Excel's sharing features are instrumental. They facilitate a smooth passage of information across individuals and teams, enhancing collective productivity.

Sharing via Cloud Services

With services like OneDrive or SharePoint, you can upload your workbook and share it directly with your colleagues. By sharing a link, you provide others with the latest version of the document, ensuring everyone works on the most current data, effectively synchronizing your efforts like musicians in an orchestra.

Real-Time Collaboration

Excel now supports real-time collaboration. This means that multiple users can edit a workbook simultaneously. It is much like a group of chefs working together in a kitchen, each contributing to the preparation of a dish, resulting in a meal that's made much faster and with collaborative effort.

Exporting as PDF

For viewing consistency across different devices and platforms, exporting your Excel file as a PDF is a practical choice. This ensures that the formatting and data are preserved exactly as intended, no matter where or how the document is opened—similar to setting a photograph in a frame, protecting its appearance regardless of the setting.

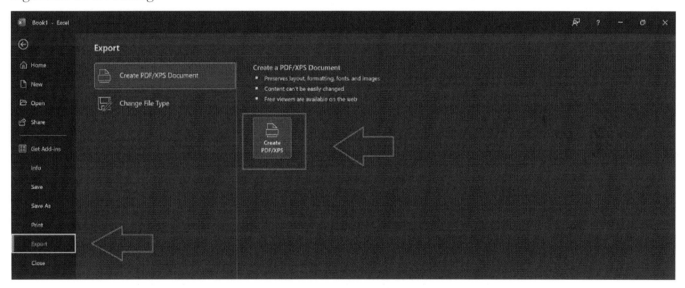

Practical Tips for Effective Document Management

Regularly Update Shared Links

If you're managing a document that is frequently updated and shared via a link, make sure to refresh and re-share the link periodically. This prevents confusion over multiple versions of a document and ensures everyone is looking at the most recent data.

Monitor Access and Permissions

When sharing files, particularly sensitive ones, keep a tab on who has access and what permissions they have. Regular reviews of access rights prevent unauthorized use and help maintain the document's integrity.

Utilize Document Version History

Most cloud storage services allow you to view and revert to previous versions of your documents. This feature is incredibly useful for tracing changes, understanding how your data evolved, and recovering from potential errors.

In mastering these techniques for saving and sharing documents in Excel, you transform your spreadsheet from a static data repository into a dynamic, secure, and collaborative tool. These practices don't just protect your data—they enhance its utility, accessibility, and reliability, empowering you to execute tasks with confidence and precision. Just as a bookshelf filled with well-preserved books serves generations of readers, well-managed Excel documents can support your professional needs continuously and reliably.

CHAPTER 2: DATA ORGANIZATION AND PRESENTATION

Welcome to the world of Excel where data isn't just about numbers and charts; it's a canvas waiting for your mastery and creativity. In Chapter 2 of *Excel Made Easy*, we embark on a crucial journey—Data Organization and Presentation. If Chapter 1 laid the groundwork, consider this chapter the framing of your data masterpiece.

Imagine walking into a room filled with scattered papers—reports here, graphs there, a sprinkle of statistics. Overwhelming, isn't it? Now picture a neatly organized space where every piece of paper is exactly where it should be, accessible and comprehensible. This is the transformation we aim for in your Excel worksheets. It's not just about making them look good; it's about making them work efficiently and effectively for you.

First, we dive into the heart of Excel spreadsheets. Here, rows and columns aren't just structural features; they are the building blocks of neat data organization. Whether you're managing inventory, planning a budget, or tracking project timelines, how you align and organize this information can drastically improve your workflow.

Next, we explore cell formatting options. I'll guide you through simple yet powerful techniques to format text, numbers, and dates. This not only improves the readability of your data but also ensures consistency, which in professional environments, is key to clear communication. Have you ever received a report where the date formats were mismatched or numbers were confusing? With a few clicks, we will eliminate that chaos from your work.

Then, the magic of conditional formatting. This feature often goes underutilized but holds the power to transform your data presentation dramatically. Conditional formatting allows you to highlight important information, differentiate data based on specific criteria, and visually scan vast amounts of data effortlessly. Think of it as setting up visual triggers that guide your eyes to the most important information without drowning in data overload.

Through easy-to-follow steps and practical real-world examples, this chapter doesn't just teach you features; it equips you with the skills to present your data compellingly and efficiently. By the end of this chapter, not only will you feel more confident in organizing your data, but you will be able to use Excel as a powerful tool that speaks clearly and persuasively in the language of organized data. Let's turn those intimidating data sets into well-structured, easy-to-navigate masterpieces.

FUNDAMENTALS OF EXCEL SPREADSHEETS

Stepping into Excel, the very first sight that greets you is a spreadsheet—a vast grid waiting to be filled with data. For many, this marks the onset of a journey, a pathway through which data becomes meaning and numbers narrate stories. In this subchapter, we are going to unwrap the fundamentals of Excel spreadsheets, turning them from daunting grids to familiar grounds where you not only navigate but master the management and organization of your data.

Understanding the Grid

At its core, an Excel spreadsheet is a matrix composed of rows and columns. Rows run horizontally and are identified by numbers (1, 2, 3, etc.), while columns run vertically, labeled by letters (A, B, C, etc.). The point where a row and a column intersect is called a cell, and it is in these cells that you input your data.

For beginners, imagine each Excel cell as a small box where you can store a piece of information. When handling Excel, every task—whether entering data, sorting a list, or creating a formula—begins by selecting one or more of these cells.

Data Entry Basics

Entering data in Excel is straightforward—click a cell, type your information, and press Enter. But the true artistry of Excel lies not in entering data but in how you organize this data. Excel isn't just about storing numbers or text; it's about making that data serve a purpose. Here's a practical tip: always think ahead about how data should be structured to facilitate analysis later. For instance, keeping all data related to a single subject in one column ensures consistency, which becomes crucial when you perform functions like sorting or applying formulas.

Efficient Navigation

Navigating through vast datasets can get cumbersome. However, Excel offers shortcuts that speed up navigation. You can jump swiftly from one edge of your data to another or swiftly scroll through long columns and rows. Learning these keyboard shortcuts early on will make your Excel use far more efficient. One helpful shortcut is using Ctrl + Arrow key: it transports your cursor to the last populated cell in any direction, enabling rapid movement across the data landscape.

Selection Techniques

Excel's power is magnified when you efficiently select cells because most operations depend on first highlighting the cells you want to work with. Whether you're applying a format, typing in functions, or setting up charts, being able to select single or multiple cells, ranges, or even entire worksheets accurately and quickly is vital. Clicking and dragging to highlight a range, holding Shift while using arrow keys for precise selection, and using Ctrl to toggle the selection of multiple ranges are some nuanced techniques that enhance workflow.

Managing Rows and Columns

Adjusting the size of rows and columns to fit your data can drastically improve readability. No one enjoys reading information that is squished or overly stretched. AutoFit is a quick solution for resizing a column or row based on its longest cell entry.

Just double-clicking the divider between the labels in your row or column header lets Excel automatically adjust the size to fit the data. Such small adjustments can make looking at your data a much more pleasant experience.

Sorting and Filtering

Sorting and filtering are two of the most fundamental capabilities in Excel that significantly enhance data usability. Imagine you have an extensive list of customer transactions. Finding all transactions above a certain value, or sorting them by date, transforms a simple list into a powerful tool for analysis. Sorting rearranges your data based on specific criteria, while filtering allows you to temporarily hide data that doesn't meet certain conditions.

Formatting for Clarity

Formatting isn't just about aesthetics; it's crucial for clarity. Applying different fonts, adjusting sizes, or changing color not only makes your spreadsheet attractive but also navigable. Highlight important data points by using bold text or color differentiation. Conditional formatting automates this process by changing the appearance of cells within a range based on your specified conditions—think of it as setting rules that visually punctuate your data depending on its values.

The Power of Formulas

One of Excel's standout features is its formula capabilities. Formulas are instructions to calculate data, and they can range from simple arithmetic like summing a column of numbers (=SUM(A1:A10)) to complex manipulations involving multiple operations. Understanding basic formulas and continuing to build on this knowledge prepares you for more advanced data tasks in later chapters.

Real-world Application

Suppose you are tasked with organizing an annual budget. Using the techniques covered—efficient data entry, proper structural organization, mastering the art of sorting and filtering, and applying basic formulas—you can not only set up your annual figures but also draw meaningful conclusions through analysis, such as identifying spending trends and forecasting future needs.

Transitioning from a spreadsheet novice to a competent user involves understanding and applying these fundamental aspects of Excel. Think of your spreadsheet as a tool not just for recording data, but for analyzing and understanding it. This approach changes your interaction with Excel from mere data entry to engagement with information that supports decision-making and insight generation. As we progress, remember that each small step mastered contributes to a larger landscape of Excel proficiency.

MANAGING ROWS AND COLUMNS

As you delve deeper into the practical realm of Excel, understanding how to manage rows and columns effectively becomes not just useful, but essential. This segment of our journey is focused on refining your spreadsheet skills, specifically honed in on the structural components of Excel—its rows and columns. The nuanced control over these elements can significantly streamline your data presentation and accuracy.

The Basics of Row and Column Management

Whenever you're working in Excel, think of rows and columns as the skeleton of your data framework. Just as bones provide structure to the body, rows and columns support your data, laying out a grid where information is stored, analyzed, and displayed. To manage them effectively, it's crucial to grasp how to adjust their size, organize them logically, and apply relevant settings to enhance readability and functionality.

Adjusting Row Heights and Column Widths

Imagine entering data that varies in length. In some cells, you might have a single word, and in others, a full sentence or more. If the row or column size doesn't accommodate this variation, your data can end up looking cramped or excessively spread out. Adjusting the height of rows and the width of columns ensures that every piece of information fits neatly in its designated space.

To adjust, simply move your cursor to the line dividing the rows or columns headers, click, and drag to resize. For a faster adjustment, double-click the divider line, and Excel will automatically resize the row or column to fit your data precisely, known as AutoFit.

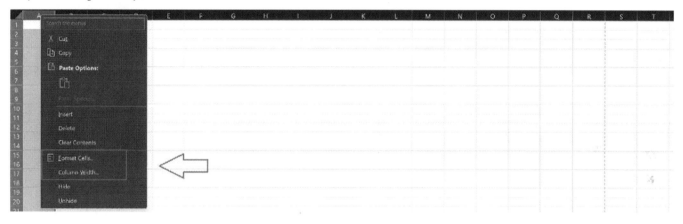

Inserting and Deleting Rows and Columns

As your datasets grow, you might need to insert additional rows and columns or remove unnecessary ones. This is common in dynamic projects where data evolves over time, such as budgeting or inventory tracking.

To insert a new row or column, right-click on a row number or column letter and select 'Insert' from the context menu. This action shifts existing rows or columns accordingly and provides a blank slate for new data. Conversely, to delete a row or column, use the right-click menu again and select 'Delete.' This helps maintain a tidy dataset by removing empty or redundant entries.

Hiding and Unhiding Rows and Columns

Sometimes, you want to focus on particular data without the distraction of other information, but you don't necessarily want to delete these rows or columns permanently. This is where hiding comes into play. By right-clicking on the row number or column letter and selecting 'Hide,' you can temporarily remove them from view, simplifying your workspace.

When you need to revisit the hidden data, you can 'Unhide' them in a similar manner. This feature is especially useful during presentations or reports where you only need to display relevant data subsets.

Grouping Rows and Columns

When dealing with complex datasets, grouping related rows or columns can greatly enhance your spreadsheet's usability. Grouping allows you to create a collapsible and expandable section in your spreadsheet, which is ideal for maintaining an organized and navigable document.

To group, select the rows or columns you wish to group, then go to the 'Data' tab on the Ribbon and click 'Group.' This functionality aids in managing detailed data without overwhelming the viewer, letting you quickly expand and collapse data sections as needed.

Practical Example: Financial Reports

Consider you are preparing a financial report that contains quarterly sales data alongside annual summaries. The detail in quarterly data is crucial but can clutter your view when analyzing annual trends. By grouping quarterly data, you can collapse it when focusing on yearly summaries, then expand it as needed for a deeper dive. This not only keeps your spreadsheet clean but also tailors it to various levels of data analysis, from detailed scrutiny to high-level overviews.

Efficiency Tips

Speed and efficiency in managing rows and columns can significantly impact your productivity in Excel. Keyboard shortcuts offer a quick way to perform many of the tasks discussed:

- To quickly adjust column width or row height to fit the data, select your columns or rows and use Alt + H, O, I for AutoFit.
- To insert new rows or columns with a shortcut, use Ctrl + Shift + + after selecting where you want to insert.

Embracing these capabilities enhances not just your efficacy but also your confidence in using Excel. By mastering row and column management, you set a strong foundation for advanced data handling, paving the way for more sophisticated operations like advanced formulas and data analysis in upcoming chapters.

Remember, each step in mastering Excel brings you closer to a profound competency that turns substantial data into impactful insights.

CELL FORMATTING OPTIONS FOR TEXT, NUMBERS, AND DATES

Diving into the details of Excel often brings us to one of its most practical, though seemingly mundane features: cell formatting. However, once you unravel its complexities, you'll discover that proper formatting for text, numbers, and dates is anything but mundane—it's transformative. It enhances clarity, accuracy, and even the aesthetic appeal of your data. Let's explore how these formatting options can make your Excel spreadsheets not only functional but also professional and easy to work with.

Formatting Text for Clarity

Text in Excel is the basic medium through which most of the data is communicated, be it titles, labels, or categorical data. The primary aim here is readability. Excel provides a vast array of text formatting tools that help make your text clear and distinguished. From choosing the right font and size to applying styles like bold or italics, each choice plays a crucial role.

For instance, consider you are setting up a spreadsheet to track customer feedback. By bolding the header row and using a clear, legible font, you instantly make the spreadsheet easier to navigate. Alignment also plays a crucial role; aligning headers to the center of cells and entries to the left can greatly increase the data's readability.

Handling Numbers with Precision

When it comes to numbers, precision and clarity are key. Excel offers specific formatting options for numbers that enable you to display values exactly how they need to be seen, whether as percentages, currency, or simple decimals.

Imagine you are preparing a financial report. Here, displaying numbers as currency with two decimal places makes the report professional and easy to interpret. Similarly, using the percentage format for ratios or growth rates instantly communicates the nature of the data without needing further explanation.

The comma style, which includes a separator for thousands, can be particularly helpful for large numbers, enhancing readability significantly.

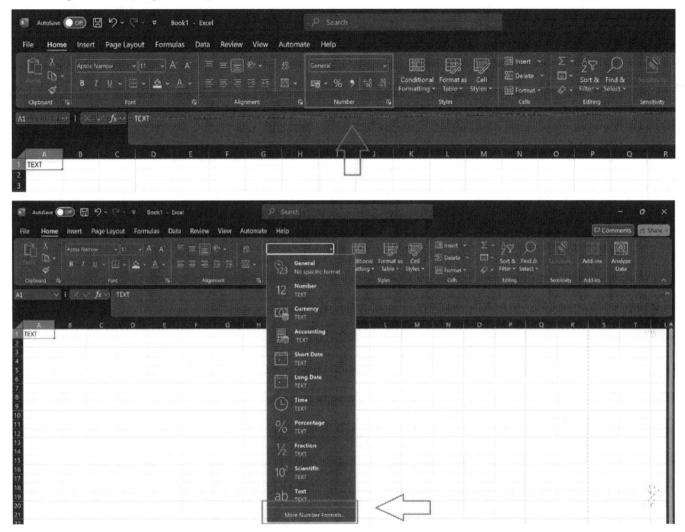

Mastering Date Formats

Dates can be tricky because of the variety of formats used globally. Excel's flexibility lets you choose from numerous date formats, ensuring that you can display dates in a way that best suits your regional setting or organizational standards.

Suppose you are managing a project timeline. The format in which you display dates, such as 'MM/DD/YYYY' or 'DD-MM-YY', can affect how quickly project milestones are understood. Beyond mere aesthetic value, correct date formatting ensures that date-driven functions (like calculating the number of days between two dates) work correctly, avoiding any costly errors in project management.

Practical Application in Real-world Scenarios

To see cell formatting in action, consider a scenario where you're analyzing sales data across different regions. Here, differentiating data using text color or highlights can quickly draw attention to key figures, like highest and lowest sales numbers. Number formats ensure that your stakeholders interpret the financial data accurately, and proper date formatting maintains consistency across reporting.

Cell Borders and Fill Colors

Another area where Excel's formatting shines is in its use of borders and fill colors. These elements can guide the eye and group related data visually. Applying a border around a set of cells helps define areas of your spreadsheet, making it easier to differentiate sections, much like chapters in a book. Fill colors can be used to indicate different types of data or just to highlight critical data points.

Conditional Formatting

For a dynamic approach to formatting, Excel's conditional formatting tool automatically applies formatting based on the rules you set. It's like setting up automatic alerts within your data. For example, you might set a rule to highlight all sales over $10,000 in green and all sales below $5,000 in red. This not only makes these figures stand out but also allows for immediate visual analysis of data performance.

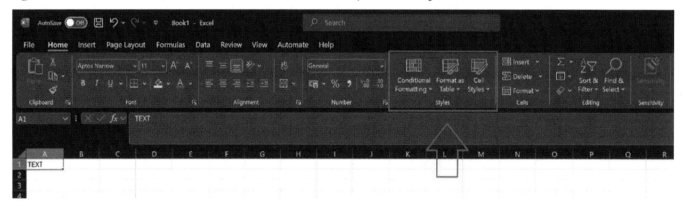

Combining Formats

Often, the most effective way to format is by combining these individual tools to suit your specific needs. Textual, numerical, and date data might require combinations of formats. For comprehensive financial reports, headers might need bold, centered text; financial figures could use currency format, and special notes might be italicized.

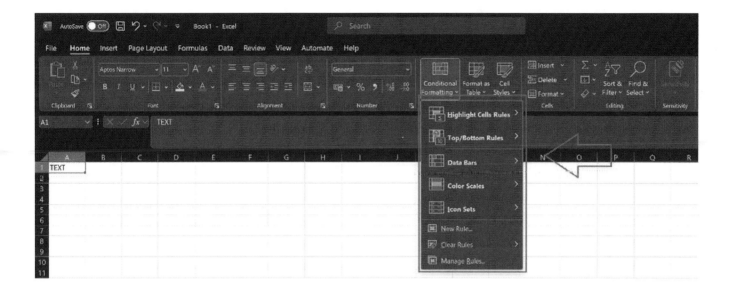

Efficiency Tips

To streamline the formatting process, remember: - Use the Format Painter to quickly apply a set format from one cell to others. - Define custom formats if the presets do not meet your needs, ensuring consistency across your document. - Practice with the cell styles available on the Home tab for quick, professional-looking results.

Proper formatting in Excel has the power to transform raw data into informative, visually appealing information streams. Whether you are preparing a report, managing a database, or creating a budget, taking the time to apply appropriate formatting settings is crucial. It's not just about making spreadsheets look good—it's about ensuring they communicate effectively, minimize errors, and speed up data analysis processes. As we move forward, keep in mind that the well-formatted data is both a pleasure to use and a powerful tool in decision-making.

IMPLEMENTING CONDITIONAL FORMATTING

One of the more dynamic and visually impactful features of Excel is conditional formatting. This tool breathes life into your spreadsheets by automatically applying specified formatting to cells based on the criteria you set. By using conditional formatting, you have a robust way to highlight significant data points, differentiate data, and create visually intuitive spreadsheets—all without manual intervention once the rules are set. Let's delve into understanding the scope and practical applications of implementing conditional formatting in Excel.

Understanding Conditional Formatting

At its core, conditional formatting changes the appearance of cells within a range based on certain conditions. This could mean changing the color of cells, applying different fonts, or even altering borders and fill depending on the data the cells contain. It is especially useful in large datasets, allowing you to quickly visualize patterns and exceptions, which are crucial for data-driven decision making.

Setting Up Basic Conditional Formatting

To initiate conditional formatting, consider a scenario where you need to track sales performance. You can set a rule to highlight all sales exceeding a certain threshold. Here's a streamlined way to set this up: 1. Select the range you want to format. 2. Navigate to the 'Home' tab and click on 'Conditional Formatting'. 3. Choose 'Highlight Cells Rules' and select 'Greater Than'. 4. Enter the value that serves as your threshold and select a formatting style. Excel will then automatically apply the chosen style to all cells exceeding the specified value.

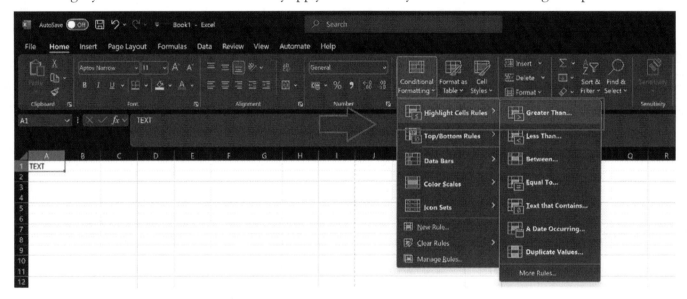

Using Color Scales

Color scales are a component of conditional formatting that assign colors to cells based on their values. This creates a heat map effect, which is exceptionally useful for spotting highs and lows at a glance. Setting up a color scale involves selecting your range and choosing 'Color Scales' from the conditional formatting options. You can pick from predefined gradients or customize your own, depending on your data visualization needs.

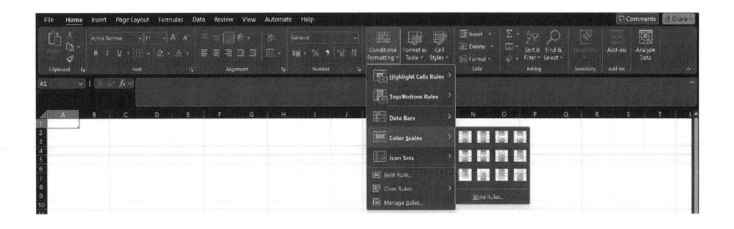

Data Bars and Icon Sets

Data bars extend across cells proportionally to the cell's value compared to the rest of the selected range, offering a quick visual representation of value differences. Similarly, icon sets can add symbols like arrows, shapes, and ratings to quickly communicate information about the data: rising trends, attention-needed areas, or tier rankings, for example.

To apply data bars or icon sets: 1. Select your desired data range. 2. From the 'Conditional Formatting' menu, choose 'Data Bars' or 'Icon Sets'. 3. Select a style that matches your visualization goals. Excel will immediately display the bars or icons in the cells, providing a quick graphical representation of the data.

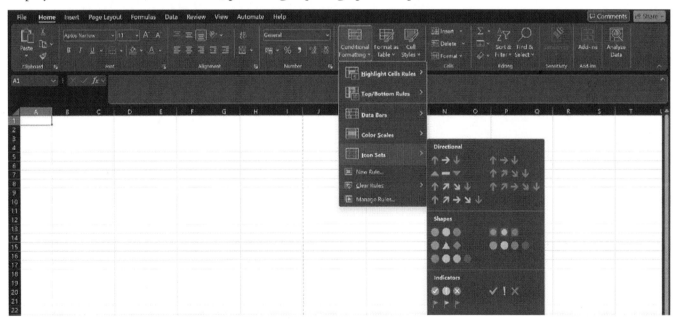

Managing and Editing Rules

A key aspect of mastering conditional formatting is managing the rules effectively. Excel allows you to view all active rules in 'Manage Rules' under the conditional formatting dropdown. Here, you can edit existing rules, change their order of precedence, or delete them as needed. This management is crucial as your dataset grows or changes.

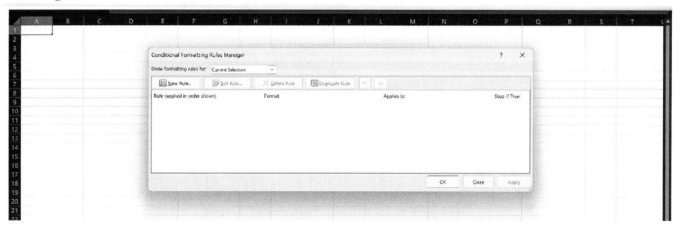

Practical Example: Risk Assessment

Imagine using Excel to assess risk in project management. You might set up conditional formatting to automatically color-code risks based on likelihood: - Low (Green) - Medium (Yellow) - High (Red)

This instantaneous visual cue helps project managers focus attention where it's needed most, enhancing responsiveness and strategic decision-making.

Tips for Effective Use

- Always ensure your data is clean and well-organized before applying conditional formatting, as disorganized data can lead to misleading visual cues.
- Use contrasting colors for more effective visual impact but be mindful of color blindness accessibility issues by choosing distinct colors and adding texture or symbols.
- Limit the use of different formats to avoid cluttering your spreadsheet, which can reduce readability instead of enhancing it.

Conditional formatting is not just about making data pretty—it's a powerful analytical tool that, when used correctly, can transform rows of raw data into a clear, concise, and immediately understandable narrative. Whether tracking sales, assessing project risk, or any other data-intensive task, conditional formatting equips you with the means to highlight what's important, focus on outliers, and visually analyze data at a glance. As you become more familiar with these tools, you'll find your ability to interpret and react to data greatly enhanced, turning Excel from a mere spreadsheet application into a dynamic dashboard of insights.

CHAPTER 3: BEGINNER DATA MANAGEMENT STRATEGIES

Welcome to Chapter 3: Beginner Data Management Strategies. As you begin to feel more comfortable with the basic functionalities of Excel, it's time to delve into how we organize and manage data more effectively. Think of Excel as your digital filing cabinet where precision and efficiency transform the overwhelming into the understandable.

At first glance, Excel might appear straightforward—rows, columns, and cells filled with data. However, the magic of Excel lies in its capacity to make this data work for you. Here, we will explore the initial steps toward mastering data management—simple yet powerful techniques to organize your worksheets in a way that augments readability and efficiency.

Let's imagine you are tasked with maintaining sales records. Initially, all information seems critical and deserves attention, but soon you'll find that sorting these details cleverly will save you much time and confusion. We'll start by using basic sorting and filtering options, allowing you to prioritize or find specific datasets effortlessly. For example, sorting may help you view products alphabetically or sales figures from high to low, bringing instant clarity to top performers or areas needing attention.

Another focus in this chapter is the practical use of grouping and ungrouping techniques. If you think about your data as chapters in a book, grouping allows you to collapse information you don't immediately need, simplifying your view and enabling you to expand it when necessary. This method helps in navigating vast arrays of data, reducing it to manageable 'chunks'.

We'll also introduce you to creating custom autofill lists—a lifesaver when it comes to data entry. No more manually typing days of the week over and over. With custom lists, you can automate these mundane aspects, focusing on analysis and decision-making.

Lastly, we will ensure you are adept with data import and export procedures, which let you communicate seamlessly between Excel and other applications or databases. Whether you're consolidating monthly reports or sharing data with colleagues, mastering this process marks a significant step in enhancing your workplace productivity.

As we journey through this chapter, remember that these strategies are not just about learning features; they're about turning Excel from daunting to doable, from just another software to your daily productivity ally.

BASIC METHODS FOR SORTING AND FILTERING

In the expansive sea of numbers and data that Excel can hold, knowing how to sort and filter this information effectively is akin to being an adept navigator, steering swiftly through a maze of information to reach your needed insight without unnecessary delay. Think about it: whether it's a list of hundreds of employees, an extensive inventory, or a yearly financial dataset, finding and organizing this data meaningfully can transform chaos into clarity and action.

Let's begin with **sorting**—a fundamental aspect that arranges your data into a meaningful order, making the analysis simpler and more intuitive. Imagine you have a sales record for the entire year detailed with information about products, sales figures, dates, and customers. With sorting, you can effectively rearrange this data to reflect items in order of highest to lowest sales, categorize it by product name alphabetically, or sort it by date to observe the sales evolution throughout the year.

To sort data in Excel, you firstly need to decide whether you want a simple, one-level sort or a more complex, multi-level sort: 1. **Single-Level Sort**: You can quickly sort a column by selecting any cell in the column you want to sort and going to the Data tab and clicking either 'Sort A to Z' or 'Sort Z to A'. This arranges your data either in ascending or descending order. 2. **Multi-Level Sort**: To see how to use Excel more powerfully, consider you want to sort the sales data not just by the sales figure but, within the same sales figures, also by date or product name. For this, Excel allows you to add levels to your sorting. Simply go to the Data tab, click on 'Sort', and then add layers to your sorting criteria according to your needs.

Now, onto **filtering**, which allows you to view only the data that meets certain criteria, effectively hiding the rest. When you're managing a large dataset, such as a membership list for a community group or product listings in an inventory, filtering can quickly show you just the members from a certain city or products of a specific category without altering your dataset.

Applying a filter in Excel is straightforward: - Begin by selecting the range of data or the columns you want to filter. - Navigate to the Data tab and click on 'Filter'. You'll see dropdown arrows appear in the header row. - Click the dropdown arrow in the column header to display a list where you can select checkboxes next to the items you want to display and deselect the items you wish to hide.

Filters can be particularly dynamic when combined with other functions. For example, you can use number filters to display sales that are greater than a certain threshold, or use date filters to see records from a specific period.

Consider an instance where a school administrator wants to view only the records of students who have registered for a new term. By applying a filter to the registration date column, the administrator could quickly isolate these records from a broader dataset of all current students.

To enhance your workspace management, Excel provides the convenience of removing all applied filters at once by selecting the 'Clear' option under the Data tab, which will return your worksheet to its original unfiltered state.

However, both sorting and filtering share a limitation—while they organize and simplify visibility, they do not change the underlying data. This limitation is crucial to bear in mind as it preserves your data integrity while allowing diverse views through different lenses.

Finally, combining both sorting and filtering allows for efficient data management. Imagine you are a project manager looking at a task list with deadlines, status updates, and responsibilities. By first filtering to show only 'Active' tasks and then sorting by 'Deadline', you effectively prioritize your immediate attention and action.

This integration of sorting and filtering in Excel does not just make data management seem less daunting but turns it into a strategic ally in your day-to-day tasks, paving the way for insightful decisions and organized workflows. By mastering these skills, you harness the full potential of Excel to not just store data, but to elevate information into a powerful tool for understanding and action. This foundation sets you up perfectly for more complex data management strategies, ensuring your growth in Excel continues confidently and competently.

WORKSHEET ORGANIZATION: GROUPING AND UNGROUPING TECHNIQUES

Mastering Excel involves more than just data entry; it's about efficiently organizing that data so you can handle it with ease and know exactly where every piece of information is when you need it. One of the less heralded but incredibly useful features of Excel that aids in organization is the ability to group and ungroup rows and columns.

Imagine you're working with a budget for a large event. Your spreadsheet might include line items for different categories like venue, catering, marketing, and miscellaneous expenses, each with subcategories. The ability to group these rows will not only make your worksheet neater but also give you control over the level of detail presented at any given time.

The Art of Grouping

Grouping in Excel lets you condense large amounts of data under a common header, which you can then expand or collapse as needed. This feature is invaluable when you are dealing with extensive datasets where you only need to review summary information or specifics occasionally.

To group rows or columns: 1. First, select the rows or columns you want to group. For instance, if you have details about catering that span rows 5 through 10, highlight these rows. 2. Go to the Data tab on the Ribbon. 3. In the Outline group, find the 'Group' button and click it. Choose 'Group...' from the drop-down menu. 4. Excel will add a small icon in the margin next to these rows or columns, which allows you to collapse or expand them with a single click.

This functionality not only keeps your spreadsheet uncluttered but also allows you to focus or present only the relevant data during meetings or reviews.

Mastering Ungrouping

As useful as grouping is, there might be times when you need to remove these groups to rearrange data or simplify the worksheet for sharing. The process for this is just as straightforward.

To ungroup: 1. Select the grouped rows or columns. 2. Head back to the Data tab. 3. In the Outline group, click on 'Ungroup' and select 'Ungroup' in the dropdown menu.

For more extensive datasets, where multiple groups exist, Excel offers the option to clear all grouping at once using 'Clear Outline', which can be a tremendous time-saver.

Practical Scenarios

To give you a real-world context, consider a sales report that includes daily, monthly, and quarterly sales data for multiple products. By grouping daily sales under each month and further grouping months under each quarter, you facilitate a top-down analysis approach. You can quickly expand the quarterly data to see monthly summaries or drill down to daily details when needed.

Another scenario could involve managing employee information where details such as contact information, employment history, and current projects for each employee are grouped. This method helps HR professionals to keep their spreadsheets clean and retrieve only the necessary data as needed.

Enhancing Grouping with Subtotals

While grouping and ungrouping offer a manual method to organize and view data, using the Subtotal feature in Excel can automate this process based on specific data points. For instance, if you're working with a spreadsheet that lists numerous transactions over several months: 1. Sort your data by the month. 2. Select the data range and navigate to Data > Subtotal. 3. Choose the column to subtotal on and the type of calculation - sum, average, count, etc., you wish to apply.

Excel will automatically group the data by month (or your chosen category), inserting a subtotal at each change in month and adding a grouped outline to your worksheet.

Tips for Effective Grouping

- **Clearly label each section** before grouping to ensure that when the sections are collapsed, it's easy to understand what each group represents.
- **Use the Group and Outline settings** to set the default expanded or collapsed state for each group.
- **Remember to refresh groups and subtotals** if data changes or if rows/columns are added or deleted.

Understanding the functionalities like grouping and ungrouping in Excel provides control over how much information you manage at once. This control can significantly enhance not only your ability to keep your worksheets clear and useful but also your overall productivity by saving time during data analysis and review sessions. With these techniques, your journey from becoming comfortable with basic Excel functionalities to mastering complex organizational strategies becomes smoother and more efficient.

DEVELOPING CUSTOM AUTOFILL LISTS

In the wonderful world of Excel, one of the most satisfying time-savers you can employ is the use of autofill. While the default autofill options in Excel cover many common scenarios, like populating dates or days, developing custom autofill lists can propel your efficiency into new realms, particularly when you're dealing with repetitive data unique to your personal or professional life.

Understanding Autofill

Excel's autofill feature allows you to automatically populate cells with a sequence of numbers, texts, or even dates without manually entering each one. It recognizes patterns and automatically fills the remaining cells accordingly. For instance, if you drag down a cell containing "January," Excel will fill the subsequent cells with the remaining months.

The Limitation of Default Autofill

While the default autofill is robust for general tasks, its presets might not always align with your specific needs. For example, suppose you are a project manager who needs to repeatedly enter a list of task statuses like "Not Started," "In Progress," and "Completed." In such cases, customizing your autofill lists can significantly trim down your data entry time.

Creating Custom Autofill Lists

Imagine you're working on a project involving numerous components repeatedly referred to in your spreadsheets, such as department names, locations, or specific product lines. Here's how you can create an autofill list tailored just for these items:

1. **Open Excel Options:** First, go to the 'File' tab on the Ribbon, click on 'Options,' which will open the Excel Options dialog box.
2. **Accessing Excel Options:** In the dialog box, click on 'Advanced,' then scroll down to find 'General' settings.
3. **Edit Custom Lists:** In the General settings, you'll see a button for 'Edit Custom Lists…'. Click on this button.

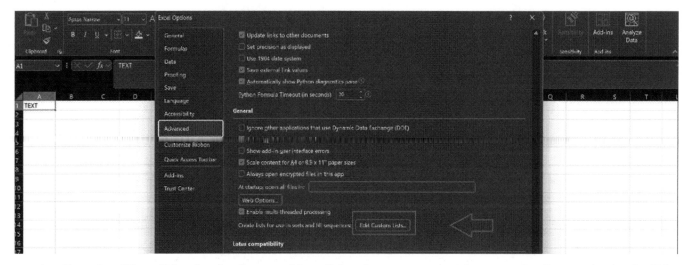

4. **Creating Your List:** In the Custom Lists dialog box, you can either type the list entries in the 'List entries' box or import the list from an existing range of cells in your workbook.

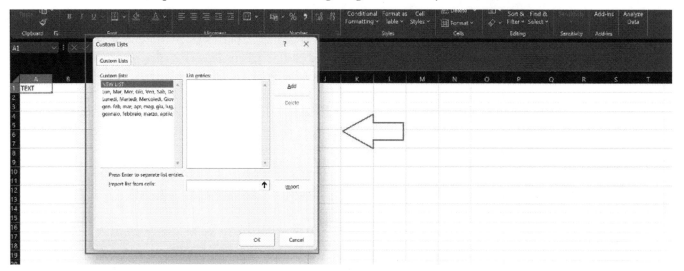

5. **Importing or Typing Entries:** If you choose to type, enter each item, pressing 'Enter' after each one to separate them. If you opt to import, use the provided input field to select the cell range containing your items.

6. **Saving Your List:** Once you have entered or selected all list items, press 'Add' and then 'OK.'

Now, when you enter the first item of your custom list in a cell and drag the fill handle (a small square at the bottom-right corner of the cell), Excel will automatically continue the list based on your custom setup.

Practical Applications

Consider a sales analyst who frequently analyzes sales by product categories such as Beverages, Condiments, Dairy Products, etc. By setting up a custom autofill list for these categories, the analyst can quickly populate these in various reports or data sheets, ensuring consistency and saving effort in the process.

Advantages of Custom Autofill Lists

- **Consistency:** Helps maintain uniformity in terminology across your worksheets, which is critical for maintaining data integrity.
- **Efficiency:** Reduces the amount of manual data entry, thus speeding up the process and reducing the risk of entry errors.
- **Customization:** Allows the flexibility to adapt Excel fully to your working style and needs, enhancing overall user experience.

Best Practices

- **Review Regularly:** Periodically review and update your custom lists to align with any changes in your project or organizational structure.
- **Limit List Size:** While it's tempting to create a custom list for everything, overly long or unnecessary lists can clutter your Excel environment. Keep them focused and relevant.
- **Educate Others:** If you work in a team environment, make sure to share relevant custom lists with your colleagues to streamline collaborative efforts.

Custom autofill lists transform a simple functionality into a powerful customization tool that adapts Excel to your specific workflows. By integrating this intelligent feature into your routine, you not only enhance your productivity but also leverage Excel's capabilities to their fullest, making your daily tasks more manageable and your time more effective. This sets a strong foundation as you advance further in managing and manipulating data within Excel.

DATA IMPORT AND EXPORT PROCEDURES

In the vast expanse of the digital age, Excel does not stand as an isolated island but rather as a bustling hub, where data constantly travels in and out, connecting with various sources and applications.

Whether you are preparing to analyze data collected from different platforms, share insights with stakeholders, or move your results into other software for further processing, mastering the art and science of data import and export in Excel is crucial.

Importing Data into Excel

Let's picture a scenario where you are a marketing analyst who needs to evaluate campaign data that's been accumulated over various platforms like Google Ads, Facebook, and email marketing tools. Each platform exports data in different formats. The challenge is to bring all this data into Excel where it can be analyzed comprehensively.

From Text Files

1. **Starting the Import**: Navigate to the 'Data' tab and select 'Get External Data'. Here, you choose 'From Text' which lets you import data from delimited files like CSV or text (.txt) files.

2. **Import Wizard**: Excel's Text Import Wizard will launch, guiding you through the steps. You'll choose the delimiter —commonly a comma or tab— that your data file uses. Excel will show you a data preview based on your selections.

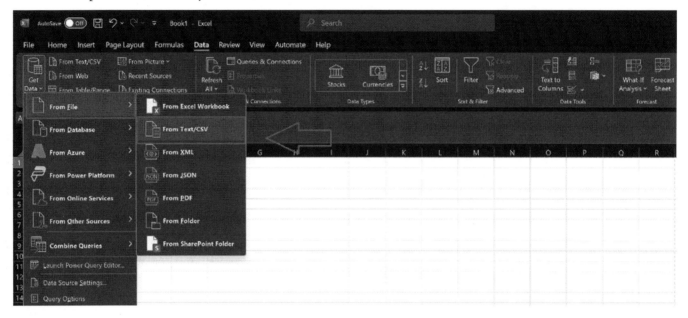

From Other Sources

For data in non-text file formats, such as from SQL databases or online services, Excel offers 'From Other Sources'. 1. **Connect to the Data Source**: Choose your data source under 'From Other Sources'. This could range from SQL Server databases to Microsoft Azure or online services. 2. **Data Retrieval**: Follow the prompts to connect to the database. You might need to enter credentials, specify the type of data you want, and how you intend to retrieve it (e.g., using a simple query or selecting from available tables).

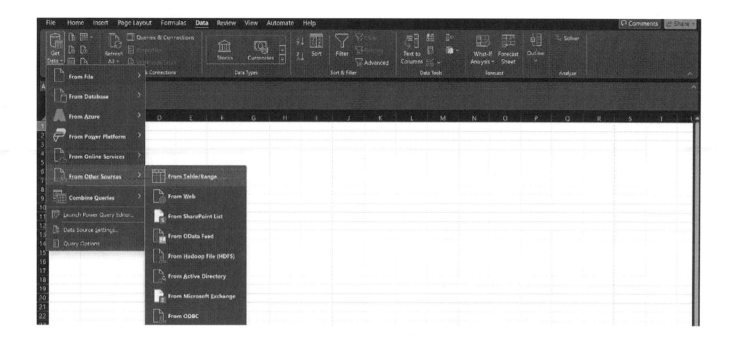

Exporting Data from Excel

Now, imagine you have completed your analysis, and you need to distribute your findings. Excel affords several ways to export your data, ensuring it can be accessed and utilized by various stakeholders no matter the platforms they use.

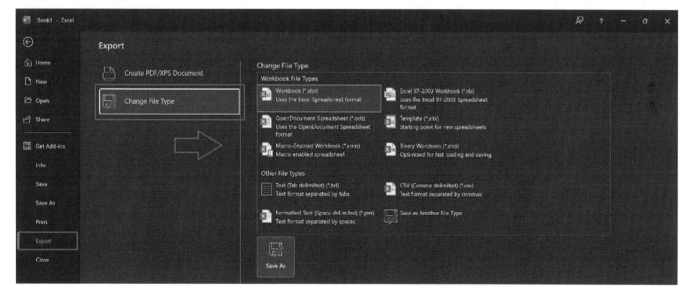

To a Text File

1. **Prepare Your Data**: Ensure that the data to be exported does not contain merged cells as these do not translate well into text formats. Check for data completeness and correctness.

2. **Save As**: Under the 'File' tab, go to 'Save As'. Select the location where you want the file saved. From the 'Save as type' dropdown menu, choose 'CSV (Comma delimited) *(.csv)' or 'Text (Tab delimited) (*.txt)*' depending on your needs.

To PDF

When you want to provide a visually intact version of your reports, exporting your Excel file to a PDF is an excellent choice. 1. **Setting Up**: Go to 'File' > 'Save As' and select 'Browse' to choose where to save the file. 2. **Export**: In the 'Save as type' drop-down, select 'PDF'. Here you can also choose if you want to export the entire workbook or just the currently selected worksheet.

Avoiding Common Pitfalls

- **Compatibility Issues**: Always ensure that the file format you import or export is compatible with the platform or software on both ends of the process.
- **Data Integrity**: Particularly with importing data, verify that no data is lost or misformatted during the transfer. Check formats of dates, numbers, and other specifics as these often end up altered.
- **Security**: When exporting sensitive data, consider encryption or password protections, particularly when using formats like PDF.

Real-World Example

Consider a small business owner who receives monthly transaction reports in CSV format from an online sales portal. By importing this data monthly, integrating it into a master Excel file and then exporting cumulative quarterly reports as PDFs to share with a financial advisor, the business owner maintains comprehensive oversight and streamlined financial planning.

The ability to seamlessly import and export data not only makes Excel a more powerful tool but transforms it into a command center for data-driven decision-making. This connectivity enables you to break down silos, integrate insights, and communicate findings effectively, ensuring that you leverage data to its full potential.

CHAPTER 4: CORE FORMULAS IN EXCEL

Welcome to the heart of Excel — formulas! As we delve into Chapter 4, it's essential to appreciate that mastering formulas is much more than a technical necessity; it's the bridge to turning raw data into meaningful information.

Imagine you're overseeing the monthly sales data for your company. You're tasked with finding patterns, understanding trends, and forecasting future growth. Without formulas, these tasks aren't just challenging; they can be downright impossible. This chapter is designed to transform you from an Excel novice to a confident user who can leverage the power of basic formulas to streamline tasks and enhance data analysis.

First, we'll introduce the bread and butter of Excel calculations: arithmetic formulas. You'll learn how to seamlessly perform operations like adding, subtracting, multiplying, and dividing using the SUM, AVERAGE, MIN, and MAX functions. This might sound straightforward, but understanding these foundations will set you up for more complex operations you'll encounter in your Excel journey.

Next, we'll tackle one of the most critical aspects of using formulas effectively — knowing the difference between relative and absolute references. This distinction might seem minor, but it's crucial for ensuring that your formulas work correctly when copied across multiple cells or when designing more sophisticated spreadsheets.

Following this, I'll take you through AutoSum, a nifty feature that not only speeds up routine calculations but also minimizes errors in your work. Figuring out sums, averages, and other calculations can be immediate with just a few clicks.

And of course, no journey into Excel formulas would be complete without addressing common errors. Know those frustrating moments when Excel spits out something unexpected? We'll decode those errors together, understand what they mean, and learn how to fix them efficiently.

By the end of this chapter, you'll have a toolkit of knowledge that enables you to craft formulas that not only compute what you need but also lay the groundwork for advanced data handling that we'll explore in later chapters. Get ready to make Excel work smarter for you, as we continue on this exciting path of discovery and efficiency.

CONSTRUCTING ELEMENTARY FORMULAS (SUM, AVERAGE, MIN, MAX)

As we dive into the world of Excel, understanding elementary formulas is your first step towards mastering this powerful tool. These basic functions, namely SUM, AVERAGE, MIN, and MAX, are not just functions; they are your initial set of tools for navigating the vast sea of data efficiently. Let's explore how these formulas can be constructed to make your data work for you, ensuring you get accurate results while saving time.

Constructing the SUM Formula: The SUM function is perhaps the most straightforward yet essential formula in Excel. It allows you to quickly add up a series of numbers. Whether you're calculating monthly expenses, daily sales, or yearly budget allocations, SUM comes in extremely handy.

Here's how you can use it: 1. Click on the cell where you want the result of your sum to appear. 2. Type =SUM(to start your formula. 3. Select the range of cells you wish to add. This could be done by clicking on the first cell in your range, holding down the shift key, and then clicking on the last cell. 4. Close your function with a parenthesis and hit Enter.

For instance, if you want to add cells A1 through A4, you would write =SUM(A1:A4). Instantly, Excel calculates the total and displays it in your chosen cell.

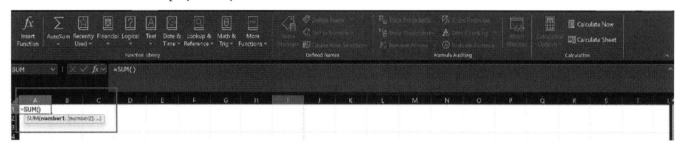

Utilizing the AVERAGE Formula: When you need to find the middle value of your data set, AVERAGE is your go-to formula. It's extremely useful for analyzing sets of numbers to find their central tendency, which can guide decisions in business, research, and even personal finance.

To calculate an average: 1. Select the cell for the result. 2. Begin with =AVERAGE(. 3. Like with SUM, select your data range. 4. Close the parenthesis and press Enter to see the result.

If analyzing test scores from B1 to B5, just type =AVERAGE(B1:B5). This simple step provides a quick glance at how well a group has performed without evaluating every single data point manually.

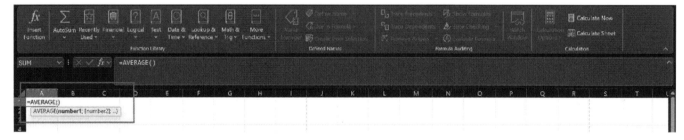

Finding Minimum with MIN Formula: Sometimes, understanding the lower end of your data spectrum is vital, especially in scenarios like checking for the minimum sales in a competitive sales report or the lowest temperatures recorded during a weather study. MIN helps you identify the smallest number in a dataset swiftly.

Applying MIN is similar: 1. Choose where you want your result to show. 2. Type =MIN(and select your range of cells. 3. Complete the formula with a closing parenthesis and press Enter.

For example, =MIN(C1:C10) will quickly scroll through cells C1 to C10 and return the smallest number among them.

Determining Maximum with MAX Formula: Conversely, the MAX function serves to find the highest value in a range of data. This can be crucial when assessing maximum sales, highest temperatures, or any other scenario where peak values are important.

To use MAX: 1. Target the cell for your result. 2. Start your formula with =MAX(, choose your range of cells. 3. Close the parenthesis and hit Enter.

Typing =MAX(D1:D10) helps you immediately identify the highest value in the range from D1 to D10.

Practical Tips and Considerations: - While selecting ranges for these formulas, ensure that there are no interruptions like blank cells or non-numeric values in numeric calculations, as they can lead to errors or skewed results. - Excel is case-insensitive in terms of function names, so typing sum or SUM works the same, though keeping it uppercase is traditional for better visibility. - Use the autofill feature by dragging the corner of the cell with the formula across other cells to apply the same calculation to other data ranges.

This is a great time-saver! - Remember, errors can often occur if the formula is not entered correctly. If you see #NAME?, double-check your formula spelling. If it's #VALUE!, check that all inputs are numbers.

Real-World Example: Imagine you're organizing a fundraising event and you've collected different amounts over several weeks leading up to the event. You might have this data sprawled across a spreadsheet. By using the SUM formula, you can quickly see total donations so far. As the event progresses, using AVERAGE could help understand typical donation sizes, and MAX might highlight the peak donation week.

By mastering these basic yet powerful formulas in Excel, you can significantly enhance your productivity and efficiency in handling data. These functions form the foundational skills that will allow you to perform more complex calculations as you progress further, making data analysis an achievable task rather than a daunting challenge.

DIFFERENCES BETWEEN RELATIVE AND ABSOLUTE REFERENCES

In the realm of Excel, mastering the concept of relative and absolute references is akin to learning how to steer your car while driving. These references are pivotal in determining how your formulas behave as you copy them across your spreadsheet. This part of your Excel learning journey is crucial, as understanding the nuances between these two types of references will not only save you time but also prevent common errors in data management.

Let's begin with **Relative References**, the default mode in Excel when you create a formula. Suppose you are working with sales data and you enter a formula in a cell to calculate the total sales for the first quarter. You might input =A2+B2+C2 in cell D2, where cells A2 to C2 contain the sales figures for January to March. Now, if you drag or copy this formula from cell D2 to cell D5, Excel automatically adjusts the formula to =A5+B5+C5. Here, Excel is understanding that you wish to perform the same operation on a different row—reflecting relative positioning. The formula changes based on the relative position of the cell where it is being copied.

While relative references are incredibly useful for many tasks, there are times when you need your formula to stick to a specific cell or range of cells, irrespective of where you copy your formula. This is where **Absolute References** come into play. They anchor your formulas to a particular location, so that no matter where you move or copy your formula, it always references the same cell(s).

Let's illustrate absolute references using the same sales data example. Imagine that you have the regional sales multiplier in cell E1, which needs to be applied to monthly sales figures across the board to adjust for regional differences. If your adjusted sales formula in F2 is =A2*E1, copying this down to F3 would typically shift the reference to =A3*E2 using relative referencing. However, E2 doesn't have the multiplier value — E1 does. To ensure the correct cell is referenced, you change the formula in F2 to =$E$1.

The dollar signs before the column letter and row number make the reference absolute, meaning copying the formula down to F3 results in =A3*$E$1, retaining the correct reference to your multiplier.

Sometimes, you might need a mixed reference where either the row or the column remains constant. This can be useful in scenarios such as applying a specific tax rate found in a particular row to various revenue figures across multiple columns. For example, if your tax rate is in cell G4 and you are calculating tax for the first month's revenue in cell B4, your formula in H4 could be =B4*$G$4. Here, only the row number in the reference to the tax rate is absolute, allowing you to copy the formula across horizontally to other months without changing the row reference.

Practical Tips and Real-World Examples: - Always double-check whether your formula requires relative or absolute referencing before copying it across. Considering the outcome first can save you debugging time later. - Use F4 key in Excel to toggle through relative and absolute references quickly when typing your formula.

This key is a handy shortcut that cycles through all combinations of relative and absolute references for the highlighted part of your formula. - A common mistake is to create unnecessarily complex formulas by overusing absolute references. Use them judiciously—only when needed to lock specific cells.

For a practical example, consider preparing a financial forecast where certain input assumptions (like growth rate, initial revenues, and expenses) are set in specific cells. Using absolute references to these assumptions in your forecast formulas allows you to freely copy your calculations across different forecast scenarios (e.g., best case, worst case) without worrying about referencing errors. This enables a streamlined approach to scenario analysis, a critical aspect in financial modeling.

By understanding and applying relative and absolute cell references correctly, you enhance your ability to manipulate data effectively in Excel. This foundational knowledge supports more complex tasks and allows you to build sophisticated and error-free spreadsheets. As you continue with Excel, remember that these references are tools in your toolkit—use them wisely to command the data at your fingertips confidently.

UTILIZING AUTOSUM FOR QUICK CALCULATIONS

In the landscape of Excel, efficiency isn't just an advantage; it's a necessity. Amid the numerous features designed to enhance your productivity, AutoSum stands out as a dynamic and powerful tool. This feature is not just about summing numbers—it's about doing it swiftly, accurately, and conveniently, making it a true ally in navigating the sea of data that modern workplaces often entail.

Imagine you're in a fast-paced environment where every second counts, perhaps an end-of-quarter review, with multiple financial sheets to reconcile. In these scenarios, AutoSum provides you with a quick way to deliver results without the tediousness of manual summation.

Unlocking the Potential of AutoSum:

AutoSum is most commonly used to perform quick summations, but its capabilities extend beyond simple addition. It can be used to automatically generate formulas for average, count numbers, min, and max functions — all essentials in data analysis.

Here's how you can harness the power of AutoSum for summing data: 1. Begin by selecting the cell where you want the result of your summation to appear. This is typically right below a column of numbers or immediately to the right of a row of numbers.

2. Next, either click on the 'AutoSum' button found in the 'Home' tab of the Excel ribbon (it resembles the Greek letter sigma, Σ) or simply press 'Alt+=' (a handy shortcut). Excel intelligently predicts the range you intend to sum based on your selection. 3. Upon clicking AutoSum or entering the shortcut, Excel automatically selects what it perceives as the adjacent range needing calculation. Check to ensure it's highlighted the correct cells. 4. Press Enter, and voilà, your sum appears.

But the magic of AutoSum doesn't stop with adding numbers. Suppose you want to find the average of a series of data points or determine the minimum or maximum value within a data set. Instead of manually inputting formulas, you can use AutoSum's drop-down menu to select the function you need.

Practical Implementations and Real-World Application:

Let's consider you are a sales manager looking at a spreadsheet containing weekly sales figures for various products. At the end of each row, you want not just the total, but also the average weekly sales, and perhaps the maximum sales in a week for each product.

1. To total the weekly sales, click in the cell at the end of the row of numbers and use AutoSum to sum across the row.
2. For calculating the average, select the next cell in the same row, click the AutoSum button, but this time, choose 'Average' from the drop-down menu. This instantly calculates the average sales per week for that product.
3. To find out the week with the highest sales, in the subsequent cell, repeat the process using AutoSum and select 'Max'.

This feature becomes particularly helpful when dealing with large datasets where manually entering formulas could be prone to errors and definitely time-consuming.

Enhanced Efficiency with Keyboard Shortcuts:

Familiarizing yourself with keyboard shortcuts can further streamline your use of AutoSum. While 'Alt+=' quickly activates the sum function, remembering 'Alt' then 'H' followed by 'U' and subsequently the specific function like 'M' for Max or 'N' for Min, can make your workflow smoother and faster.

In environments where time and accuracy are of the essence, mastering such shortcuts allows you to keep pace, ensuring data-driven decisions are based on promptly processed information.

Ensuring Accuracy in Dynamic Tables:

AutoSum also fits seamlessly into contexts involving dynamic tables or data ranges that might experience frequent changes. For example, in project management scenarios where new tasks or budget entries are continuously added, AutoSum helps maintain up-to-date totals without the need for constant manual updates.

As Excel evolves, features like AutoSum adapt, providing users not just tools for calculation but for maintaining relevance in an ever-adjusting dataset, ensuring that the figures you present or base decisions on are not just accurate but are also reflective of the latest data.

In conclusion, embracing AutoSum is less about learning a function and more about integrating a data-handling philosophy that embraces efficiency, accuracy, and adaptability. Its relevance spans industries and scenarios, proving that in a world overwhelmed by data, having the right tools to manage it is paramount. Whether you are a financial analyst, a marketing director, or a project manager, AutoSum is a feature that not only simplifies your Excel tasks but also amplifies your capability to handle data effectively and efficiently.

RESOLVING COMMON ERRORS IN FORMULAS

Navigating through Excel, it's inevitable to encounter bumps in the road, especially when dealing with formulas. These errors can be frustrating, but understanding how to resolve them is a valuable skill that enhances your proficiency. Excel provides not only the tools to identify errors but also the paths to correct them, turning potential setbacks into learning opportunities.

Understanding Error Messages

Excel is quite communicative; it tells you there's an issue with the formulas you've set up by displaying error messages. Each error type, identified by its specific code, gives clues about what's wrong. Let's break down these messages and see how to address them effectively.

#DIV/0! Error: This occurs when a formula tries to divide by zero. It's a common error in financial and operational reports where certain values expected for computation might not be available.

Resolving #DIV/0!: To handle this, you can adjust the divisor to ensure it's not zero or use the IFERROR function to set an alternative result when encountering division by zero, like so: =IFERROR(A1/B1, "No Value").

#NAME? Error: This appears when Excel does not recognize a text in your formula. Often it's due to misspelling a function name or a cell reference that does not exist.

Resolving #NAME?: Double-check the formula for misspellings. If the formula involves a function, confirm that all required arguments are specified.

#VALUE! Error: This is displayed when the wrong type of argument or operand is used. You may accidentally include a non-numeric string or a text value where a number is expected.

Resolving #VALUE!: Ensure all cells referenced in the formula contain the correct data type or use VALUE() function to convert text that represents a number into a numeric value.

#REF! Error: The #REF! message shows up if a formula refers to a cell that's not valid. This often happens after deleting a cell, row, or column used by your formula, or by pasting data over cell references.

Resolving #REF!: Check your formula to make sure all referenced cells still exist. Adjust the cell references manually if necessary.

#NUM! Error: This occurs when a formula or function contains invalid numeric values. It's a common issue when you're working with complex calculations.

Resolving #NUM!: Make sure all the numeric values are within a range acceptable for the formula, and check for data input errors. In estimating calculations, ensure that you are not providing parameters that cause the function to fail.

#N/A Error: This signifies that a value is not available to a function or formula. You might encounter this when working with Excel functions like VLOOKUP, which fails to find a match.

Resolving #N/A: Use IFERROR to handle cases where no match is found: =IFERROR(VLOOKUP(value, table, index, FALSE), "Not Found").

Practical Tips for Managing Errors

Consistent Data Entry: Ensure data used in calculations is entered consistently and accurately. Inconsistent data types are a common source of calculation errors.

Use Excel's Formula Auditing Tools: Excel offers tools like "Trace Precedents", "Trace Dependents", and "Error Checking" under the "Formulas" tab which can help you visually trace and correct errors in formulas.

Document Complex Formulas: If your workbook involves complex formulas, document these formulas either within the workbook itself using cell comments or in an accompanying document. This practice is especially helpful for troubleshooting and when you or someone else needs to understand the workflow of data.

Concrete Example

Imagine you're analyzing sales data and your spreadsheet includes a column for monthly growth percentage, calculated by dividing the difference between this month's and last month's sales by last month's sales. If last month's sales are zero (perhaps it was a new product launch), your formula will return a #DIV/0! error. By implementing an IFERROR formula, you can keep your data clean and your report aesthetically coherent.

Excel's error messages, while initially daunting, are stepping stones to achieving mastery in this powerful tool. By learning to interpret and resolve these errors, you not only enhance your problem-solving skills but also ensure your data integrity remains uncompromised. Each error resolution enriches your Excel toolkit, enabling you to tackle more complex data challenges confidently.

BOOK 2: DEVELOPING INTERMEDIATE EXCEL CAPABILITIES

CHAPTER 5: ENHANCED FORMATTING AND PERSONALIZATION

Imagine walking into a room that's been tailored just for you, where everything is arranged not only to function perfectly but also to appeal to your style and preferences. This feeling of tailor-made design is pivotal when transitioning into the intermediate capabilities of Excel, particularly when it comes to formatting and personalization — features that make your workbook not just functional but visually compelling and easier to navigate.

As we delve into Chapter 5 of "Developing Intermediate Excel Capabilities," we shift our focus from mere functionality to aesthetic finesse and user ease. Think about this chapter as your guide to making Excel not just work well but also look great and resonate with how you think and process information. Much like arranging furniture in a room, the way we format and personalize our Excel worksheets can greatly influence both the usability and the experience of the users.

You might wonder why Excel's visual and structural customization matters as much as its computational abilities. Consider the last presentation or report you prepared. How was it received? Often, the clarity and visual impact of data presentation can be just as crucial as the data itself. By enhancing formatting and personalization, you can drive attention to key areas, make your data more comprehensible, and, ultimately, more actionable.

In this chapter, we'll explore how themed formatting and styles can bring a consistent and professional look to your workbooks. You'll learn the secrets of freezing panes and splitting views that make navigating large worksheets a breeze, without losing sight of crucial headers or data points. We'll also unravel the smart tricks behind effective table customization, which aren't just about colors and fonts but are essential tools for readers to understand complex data at a glance.

And for those moments when too much information becomes a clutter, we'll tackle techniques for hiding and revealing data in your worksheets efficiently. This doesn't just clean up your space; it also focuses your audience's attention where it matters most.

By the end of this chapter, your Excel skills will not only perform tasks but will do so in a manner that is as personalized and efficient as possible. Let's elevate your Excel spreadsheets from mere data holders to compelling narratives that speak with visual impact and personal flair.

APPLYING THEMES AND STYLES FOR VISUAL CONSISTENCY

Imagine for a moment that you've just finished a stunning piece of artwork. Now comes the crucial part—choosing the right frame to complement your creation. In Excel, the 'Themes' and 'Styles' features serve a similar purpose, helping you frame your data so that it not only stands out visually but also communicates more effectively.

Why Themes Matter in Excel

Think of themes as the overarching design decisions that govern the look of your entire workbook. Excel offers a variety of built-in themes—each one includes coordinated sets of fonts, colors, and effects. By selecting a theme, you ensure consistency across your document, which not only looks professional but also aids in the readability of your content.

Let's say you're preparing a quarterly sales report. Choosing a sleek, professional theme with muted colors can make the report appear more polished and accessible. Contrast this with using a mismatch of colors and fonts, which can distract and even confuse the reader.

Applying a theme in Excel is straightforward: 1. Open your workbook and head to the 'Page Layout' tab. 2. Click on 'Themes' and browse through the available options. 3. Select a theme that resonates with the tone of your data. For a financial report, you might opt for the 'Corporate' theme, offering clean lines and a professional palette.

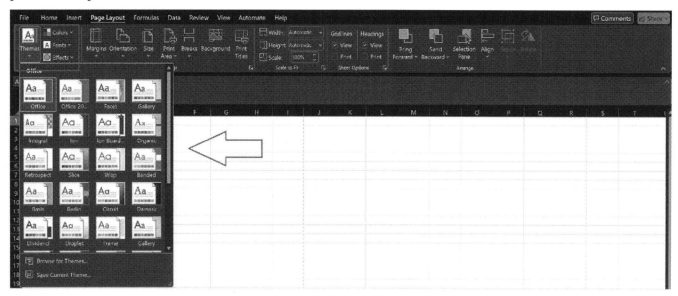

Customizing Themes for Personal Touch

Sometimes, the standard themes might not perfectly match your organization's branding or the specific mood you're trying to convey. Excel allows you to tweak these themes to better suit your needs: - **Adjust theme colors**: Customize the set of colors used on charts, texts, and cells. This is perfect for matching your company's logo or campaign theme.

- **Change theme fonts**: Opt for a different set of heading and body text fonts to change the document's character. - **Alter theme effects**: Modify how certain visual elements appear, like shadows and lines in charts.

The Role of Styles in Data Presentation

While themes provide a macro level consistency, styles deal with micro adjustments that enhance specific parts of your spreadsheet. Excel's cell styles can be likened to brush strokes on a painting, defining the appearance and feel of individual cell data.

Consider you have a table of data showing sales figures across different states. Here's where cell styles play a role. You might use a bold style for column headers, a different style for emphasis on the highest and lowest numbers, or a numeric style for aligning dollar amounts.

Applying styles is simple: 1. Highlight the cells you want to style. 2. Navigate to the 'Home' tab. 3. In the 'Styles' group, select 'Cell Styles.' 4. Choose from numerous pre-defined styles or create your own to make certain data stand out.

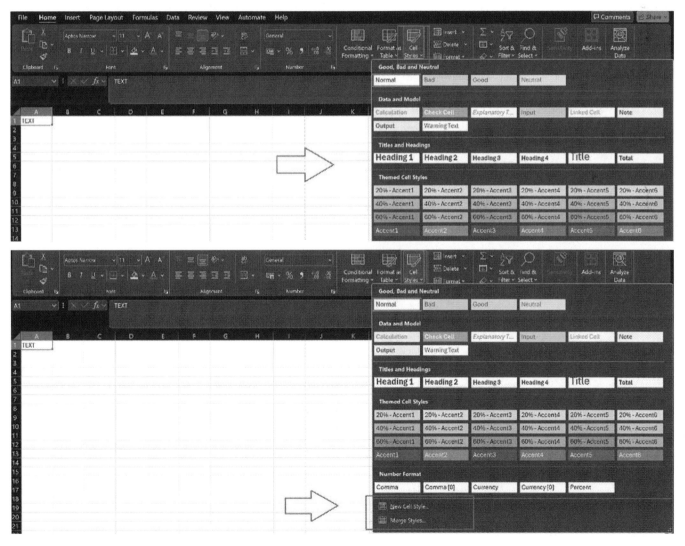

Practical Tip: Keep It Consistent

The key to effectively using themes and styles is consistency. Random changes in fonts, colors, or cell styles can make your spreadsheet hard to read and look unprofessional. Always preview your changes to see how they affect the readability and visual output of your data.

Real-World Application: Sales Reporting

Imagine you are a sales manager looking to present annual results. You select a theme that reflects your corporate colors, adding an instant visual connection to your brand. Next, you apply specific cell styles to draw attention to key metrics like annual growth and region-specific performances. This not only makes the report attractive but also directs viewer attention strategically to the most critical data.

Efficient Workflow: Themes and Styles

Incorporating themes and styles not only beautifies your workbook but also streamlines the creation process. With predefined settings, you don't need to manually format each element, saving time and maintaining consistency. Whether you're cranking out financial reports, managing inventory, or tracking project timelines, these tools help maintain a clean, readable, and engaging dataset.

As you continue to work with themes and styles, you'll start to see which combinations work best for different types of data presentations. Experiment with them according to the context of your work—what is effective for a financial report might not suit a marketing presentation. The flexibility and customization offered by Excel allow you to craft precisely tailored documents that speak clearly and beautifully of your data's story. This is how you turn raw numbers into compelling narratives that can influence and inform.

TECHNIQUES FOR FREEZING PANES AND SPLITTING VIEWS

Navigating through large Excel workbooks filled with rows of data and various columns can often feel like trying to find your way through a crowded city without a map. This is where techniques like freezing panes and splitting views come into play, acting much like navigational tools that help you keep your bearings in complex spreadsheets.

The Magic of Freezing Panes

Imagine you're reviewing a financial spreadsheet with hundreds of rows and numerous columns. As you scroll down, the headers disappear from view, leaving you to guess which column corresponds to which data type. To maintain your bearings, you can "freeze" these critical rows at the top or columns on the side of your worksheet so they remain visible as you scroll through the rest of your data.

How to Freeze Panes: A Step-by-Step Guide 1. First, decide what you need in view. If it's the top row and the first column, navigate your cursor to cell B2. This is because Excel will freeze rows and columns based on the cell you select. 2. Go to the 'View' tab in the ribbon. 3. Click on 'Freeze Panes' in the Window group. 4. You'll see three options: Freeze Panes, Freeze Top Row, and Freeze First Column. - Select 'Freeze Panes' if your cursor is in B2 to lock both the first row and the first column. - Choose 'Freeze Top Row' or 'Freeze First Column' if you only need to lock one or the other.

Splitting Views for Comparative Analysis

Now, let's talk about splitting views. This feature is akin to having multiple viewing windows open on your computer screen, allowing you to look at different sections of the same document simultaneously. It's particularly useful when you want to compare the details in distant rows or columns without having to scroll back and forth.

The Steps to Splitting Your Worksheet View 1. Open your workbook to the sheet you wish to split. 2. Position your cursor in the cell where you want to split the view. If you place it in cell C3, Excel splits the window into four quadrants. 3. Click on 'Split' in the 'View' tab under the Window group. You'll see the screen divide into separate panes which can be scrolled independently.

Both freezing panes and splitting views can dramatically increase your efficiency when working with large datasets. However, they serve slightly different purposes and are used in varying scenarios:

- **Freezing panes** is best used when you need certain rows or columns always to be visible as you navigate through your spreadsheet.
- **Splitting views** is ideal when you need to compare or refer to different sections of your workbook without continuously scrolling.

Practical Examples in Real-World Scenarios

Scenario 1: Monthly Expense Tracking Let's say you are managing a year-long project with monthly expense entries. Your spreadsheet spans across many rows, one for each day, and several columns indicating different types of expenses. By freezing the top row(s) that contain your headers and the first column that includes the date entries, you can scroll through your monthly expenses while constantly viewing which data belongs to which category and date.

Scenario 2: Employee Performance Review In a spreadsheet where you keep records of employee performance metrics, imagine you have the employees' names in the first column and various performance indicators across the first row. Here, you might decide to split the view horizontally to keep an overview on the first row while scrolling through individual records. This makes side-by-side comparisons straightforward without losing sight of the metrics.

These advanced navigation tools in Excel do not just serve as mere convenience features; they're powerful enhancements that can transform how you manipulate and interact with data. Whether you are a finance professional working with elaborate budget spreadsheets or a human resources manager handling extensive employee databases, mastering these tools allows for smoother, more effective data management.

By integrating these practices regularly, you ensure your workbook is not just a container of data but a dynamic layout that responds to your interactive needs, making data analysis not only more manageable but also more enjoyable. As you progress through Excel, these skills will continue to build a foundation for more advanced data management techniques, enabling you to handle complex datasets with confidence and precision.

DESIGN AND APPLICATION OF TABLE FORMATTING

When you're working with data in Excel, organizing it into a table format isn't just about making it look good—it's about adding structure and functionality, which in turn, enhances your ability to analyze and manage the data effectively. This approach turns your data into a dynamic and interactive database.

Understanding Table Design Philosophy

Creating a table in Excel is like building the framework for a house. Just as the framework defines the structure of a home, so too does table formatting help define and organize your data. The beauty of Excel tables isn't just in their ability to hold data, but also in their enhanced functionality, which includes improved sorting and filtering options, and features like automatic formula updates and total rows.

Applying Table Formatting: A Simple Guide 1. Begin with your data range; whether it's a few rows or thousands, Excel tables can handle it. Navigate to the 'Insert' tab on the Ribbon and select 'Table'. Ensure that your data range is correctly selected and check the box that reads 'My table has headers' if your data includes headers. 2. Once the table is created, you'll notice that Excel automatically applies a default style—but don't stop there. You can change the table style to better suit your data or presentation needs. Excel offers a range of built-in styles, accessible from the 'Design' tab under 'Table Tools'. Here, you can choose different colors, banded rows, and other features to enhance readability and visual appeal.

Advanced Features in Table Design

Excel tables pack some powerful features under the hood. One such feature is the automatic expansion of tables. Add a new data point in the row immediately below your table, and Excel includes it in the table, formats it according to the table style, and extends any formulas from above columns. This means your data analyses are always up-to-date, which is particularly helpful in reports or dashboards.

Creating Calculated Columns: When you enter a formula in one table cell, Excel can automatically fill the formula down the entire column. This smart feature saves time and ensures consistency in your calculations. For instance, if you have sales data and you need to calculate the tax for each transaction, simply type the tax calculation formula in the first cell of the new column, and Excel fills it downward for all existing entries.

Table Tools for Enhanced Data Management

The real power of Excel tables lies in their built-in tools that simplify data management. The 'Design' tab in 'Table Tools' is where much of this functionality resides.

- **Sort and Filter:** This is more intuitive in tables with dropdown arrows appearing next to each column header.

- **Total Row:** Quickly add a row at the bottom of your table that can be customized to sum up data, find averages, or other aggregate functions.

- **Slicer:** Introduced in later versions of Excel, slicers are visual tools that allow you to quickly filter table data. They are especially useful in dashboards or other reports where quick, dynamic filtering of data is beneficial.

Concrete Example: Sales Data Analysis

Imagine you manage sales data for a multinational corporation. Each day, hundreds of transactions populate your dataset. By formatting this data into a table, you can use slicers to see which products are performing best in real-time, sort data to prioritize high-value customers, and use the total row to summarize daily sales or calculate commissions. This immediate access to organized data isn't just about seeing numbers; it's about making informed business decisions fast.

From Data to Insight

Applying table formatting in Excel transforms columns and rows of data into an organized database ready for analysis and reporting. In your ongoing use of Excel, you'll find that tables not only save time but also open up new possibilities for taking raw data and turning it into actionable insights.

Whether you're preparing a report for the next board meeting, managing payroll, or tracking inventory, understanding and using Excel's table formatting tools effectively can significantly enhance your productivity and decision-making efficiency.

As you master these skills, you'll move from simply entering data into Excel to commanding it to deliver deeper business intelligence. This transition is what places Excel as a fundamental tool in business operations across global industries.

TECHNIQUES FOR HIDING AND REVEALING DATA

Navigating through comprehensive data sets in Excel often means dealing with sections of data that either clutter the view or are simply irrelevant at certain times. The ability to hide and unhide this data, without altering the integrity of your overall dataset, empowers users by providing a cleaner workspace. Excel provides several nuanced techniques for managing the visibility of your data to tailor your worksheets not just to your needs, but also to the audience or situation at hand.

Streamlining Data Views Through Hiding Techniques

Let's explore a common scenario: you have an exhaustive annual financial report it's brimming with monthly, quarterly, and regional breakdowns. During a conference call, you want to focus only on the annual summary without navigating through the clutter of extensive data. This is where Excel's hiding features become crucial.

Hiding Rows and Columns 1. To hide less pertinent rows or columns individually, simply right-click on the row or column number you wish to hide and select 'Hide' from the context menu. This makes the row or column disappear temporarily from the view, though the data still exists and is accounted for in any calculations. 2. When you need to reveal them, right-click on the identifiers of the rows or columns adjacent to the hidden ones and choose 'Unhide'.

Hiding Sheets Occasionally, you might have entire sheets that are useful for background calculations or data entry but are not needed for presentation or consolidated analysis: 1. Right-click on the sheet tab you wish to hide. 2. Select 'Hide', and the sheet will vanish from view, leaving a more navigable set of tabs. 3. To bring it back, right-click on any sheet tab, choose 'Unhide', and then select the sheet you want to make visible again.

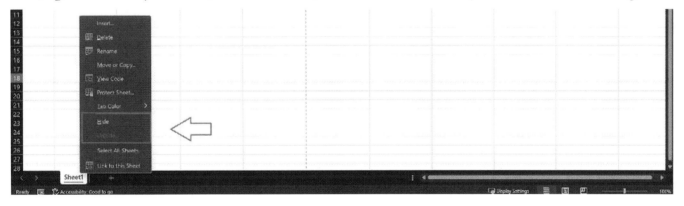

Advanced Technique: Custom Views for Dynamic Data Management

For those who regularly toggle between different data views depending on the task at hand or the audience, Excel's Custom Views feature is a game-changer.

Creating a Custom View 1. Adjust your worksheet to show only the data you want visible in a particular view — this might include scrolled positions, filter settings, and hidden columns or rows. 2. From the 'View' tab, click on 'Custom Views'. 3. Click 'Add', give your view a name, and specify whether it should save print settings and hidden rows/columns. 4. Now, whenever you need to switch perspectives, return to 'Custom Views' and select the desired preset view.

Practical Usage: Financial Reporting

Imagine you're preparing a quarterly financial report for senior management. They are particularly interested in high-level insights and not the underlying details. You could create a custom view that hides the granular monthly breakdowns but shows a summary sheet with key metrics and trends. During presentations, with a click, your Excel workbook transforms into a clear, concise, and effective report tailored perfectly to upper management's needs.

Best Practices for Hiding Data Responsibly

It's vital when hiding data to remember two key points: - **Document your hidden data**: Always keep track of what data is hidden and why. This can be managed in a documentation sheet or external document to prevent confusion or misinterpretation especially when sharing the workbook. - **Check calculations**: Ensure that hidden data is accounted for correctly in summaries or calculations. Accidental omission can lead to incorrect results and decisions based on them.

Crafting Intuitive, User-focused Spreadsheets

By harnessing Excel's various techniques for hiding and revealing data, you enhance not only the aesthetics of your spreadsheets but also their functionality. This allows for presentations that are not only more focused but also more relevant to the specific audience. Whether it's streamlining key data points during a high-stakes meeting or organizing vast arrays of information into digestible segments, understanding and utilizing these strategies will elevate your proficiency and presentation in Excel, often transforming overwhelming datasets into clear, actionable insights.

CHAPTER 6: ANALYZING DATA WITH EXCEL

Welcome to Chapter 6: Analyzing Data with Excel. As you've grown more comfortable with Excel through the basic functions and intermediate features detailed in earlier chapters, you're now stepping into a pivotal arena—data analysis. Here, the true power of Excel begins to shine, transforming raw data into actionable insights.

Data analysis in Excel isn't just a process—it's your secret weapon in the professional world. With the tools you're about to learn, you can pivot from being merely data-informed to data-driven. Imagine preparing for a crucial meeting, armed not just with numbers, but with visually compelling insights that tell a compelling story of trends, challenges, and opportunities. Excel equips you to achieve just that, and this chapter is where you start.

First, we delve into Pivot Tables—Excel's powerhouse for summarizing large sets of data without writing complex formulas. If you've ever been daunted by extensive spreadsheets that seem to drown valuable information in a sea of numbers, Pivot Tables will become your new best friend.

Next, we'll explore how you can enhance your data interpretation with advanced filtering and slicing techniques within your Pivot Tables. This isn't just about seeing your data; it's about seeing through your data to glean the kernels of knowledge that spark decision-making.

We'll also integrate subtotals and grand totals to your analysis processes. These features might sound straightforward, but they perform the heavy lifting when summarizing data points—a must-have skill in any data analyst's toolkit.

Finally, if you've ever experienced the frustration of presenting data that doesn't get the point across, I'll show you how Pivot Charts and other visualization tools in Excel can transform your bland sheets into dynamic narratives. This isn't just about making pretty charts; it's about crafting visuals that engage, inform, and persuade.

Each step through this chapter builds not just your skills, but your confidence. It's designed for you to follow along, integrate tips practically, and see immediate results in your data tasks. Whether you're prepping data for a meeting, a report, or decision-making, mastering these techniques will mark a significant leap in your Excel journey. So let's harness these tools and turn your data into dialogues that drive success.

BASICS OF PIVOT TABLES: CONSTRUCTING YOUR INITIAL PIVOT TABLE

Imagine you're sitting at your desk staring at an overwhelming spreadsheet filled with sales data from the past year. Each row represents a transaction, and every column holds crucial bits of information like sales figures, dates, product categories, and more. There's valuable insight in this ocean of numbers—insight that could streamline operations, amplify sales, or even transform business strategy—if only you could make sense of it. This is where Pivot Tables come into play, turning your daunting data into digestible information.

Constructing Your Initial Pivot Table

Let's start by constructing our first Pivot Table. Think of this tool as your personal data assistant, ready to organize and summarize complex data without altering your original dataset. Here's how to make your first Pivot Table:

1. **Choose Your Data**: The first step involves selecting the pile of data you want to examine. This could be as vast as an entire worksheet or as specific as a certain range of cells.

2. **Inserting the Pivot Table**: Navigate to the 'Insert' tab on the Ribbon and click on 'PivotTable.' Excel will prompt you to confirm the data selection and choose whether you want the Pivot Table in a new or existing worksheet. For clarity, let's place it in a new worksheet.

3. **Defining Rows, Columns, and Values**:

   o Drag fields to the Rows or Columns areas to determine how your data will be grouped. For instance, if you're looking at sales data, you might choose "Month" for Columns and "Product Category" for Rows.

   o Next, drag a field into the Values area. This could be 'Sales Amount' to compute total sales. Excel will automatically calculate sums for numerical data or counts for text data.

4. **Adjusting Field Settings**: Sometimes, the default calculations might not suit your needs. Right-click on any value within your table, choose 'Value Field Settings,' and select the type of calculation you prefer, such as average or count.

5. **Sorting and Filtering**: Pivot Tables allow you to focus on subsets of your data. For instance, filter to view only data where sales were above a certain threshold, or sort to identify top-performing products or months.

6. **Expanding and Collapsing Groups**: Some data, when deeply nested, can appear cumbersome in a Pivot Table. Use the expand/collapse buttons to show or hide detailed data entries under each category.

Practical Tips and Considerations

- **Refreshing the Data**: As your underlying data changes, so too should your Pivot Table. Remember, the table doesn't automatically update. Right-click within the table and select 'Refresh' to ensure it reflects the latest data.

- **Design and Layout**: Under the 'Design' tab in the PivotTable Tools on the Ribbon, you can choose from various presets to enhance readability and presentation. Simple tweaks like banded rows or first-column highlights can make your data more digestible.

- **Calculated Fields**: To go a step further, add calculated fields inside your Pivot Table. For example, if you want to analyze profit margins, you can create a new field calculating the margin per transaction by using existing 'Cost' and 'Revenue' columns.

Using Real-World Scenarios

Let's apply this in a real-world situation. Consider a mid-size retail company assessing quarter-end performance. The finance team uses a Pivot Table to segment revenue by product category across different regions and compare it against cost.

Each product category and region is a row and column, respectively, with profit margin as a value. This quick visualization helps identify underperforming products or regions, guiding strategic decisions such as promotional efforts or inventory distribution.

Maintaining Clarity and Organization

As you become comfortable with Pivot Tables, you'll begin to appreciate their power and versatility. However, a common pitfall is overcomplication. Keep your Pivot Tables focused on specific insights you're seeking rather than trying to squeeze every piece of data into a single giant table. Multiple, well-organized Pivot Tables are generally more effective than a single overloaded one.

In summary, Pivot Tables are not just features of Excel; they are foundational tools for anyone looking to make data-driven decisions. By transforming raw data into structured, comprehensible formats, they allow you to unearth trends and insights that can profoundly impact your understanding and strategic direction. Whether it's boosting efficiencies, identifying growth opportunities, or simply keeping a better track of performance, Pivot Tables turn you into an architect of information, molding raw data into actionable intelligence. So, venture forth and pivot your way to data mastery!

DATA GROUPING WITHIN PIVOT TABLES

Imagine yourself back in that bustling office, staring down a massive spreadsheet, this time loaded with a different kind of dataset — perhaps sales data segmented by region, date, and product categories. Now, with a foundation in creating Pivot Tables, you're ready to elevate your analysis. Grouping data within these tables is akin to organizing a vast library by genres, authors, and publication years, making finding a specific book or spotting trends much easier. This section will guide you on grouping data effectively within Pivot Tables, transforming a sea of information into islands of insights you can easily navigate.

Understanding Grouping in Pivot Tables

Grouping in Pivot Tables allows you to consolidate similar data into groups to compare and analyze. This could be dates, numbers, or text data. You can group sales data by months into quarters, or by days into weeks, providing a structured overview of trends and patterns.

1. **Grouping Dates**: When dealing with chronologically ordered data, grouping dates can simplify analysis over time.

    For instance, rather than analyzing sales data daily, you could group data into months or quarters. Simply right-click on any date in your Pivot Table, select 'Group', and then choose the desired grouping intervals such as months, quarters, or years.

2. **Grouping Numbers**: Similar to dates, numbers can be grouped to better categorize the data. For instance, if your data spans sales figures from $1 to $1,000, grouping them into ranges (e.g., $1-100, $101-200) might make analysis more digestible. Right-click on a number within a Pivot Table, hit 'Group', and set the starting and ending points, along with the interval.

3. **Grouping Text**: While less common, text data can also be grouped. For example, if your product categories are very granular, you might want to group them into broader categories to see the bigger picture. Right-click on the text data, select 'Group', and manually group items into new segments.

Why Group Data?

Data grouping can significantly enhance readability and clarity, making the derived conclusions more apparent. For example, when data is grouped into quarters rather than months, seasonal trends may become clearer, aiding in more strategic decision-making.

Dynamic Data Grouping

Excel's dynamic grouping means any changes you make to your data range (e.g., adding extra dates) are automatically recognized in your groups when refreshed. This ensures your insights are based on the latest data without manually updating the groupings.

Handling Over-Grouping

One frequent mishap in data analysis is over-grouping — creating so many small groups that the data becomes as cluttered and hard to interpret as the ungrouped data. If you find the Pivot Table as confusing post-grouping, consider enlarging your groups or reducing the quantity of group criteria.

Real-World Example: Streamlining Company Data

Consider a company, 'EcoGoodies', that has sales representatives in over 50 cities. Analyzing performance city-wise can be cumbersome and not particularly enlightening. By grouping cities into regions (North, South, East, West), the company's management can quickly identify which regions are performing or underperforming, thereby strategizing better marketing or resource allocation based on these insights.

Refreshing Grouped Data

After grouping, always ensure to refresh your Pivot Table to reflect any recent changes to the data set. This is done by right-clicking within the Pivot Table and selecting 'Refresh'. This step is crucial to maintaining the accuracy of your analysis.

Design and Aesthetic Adjustments

After grouping, you might find it helpful to adjust the design and layout of your Pivot Table to improve readability. Consider features like 'Banded Rows' and 'Banded Columns' under the PivotTable Design tab, which can help differentiate between grouped sections visually.

Proper grouping within Pivot Tables can drastically reduce the complexity of analyzing significant datasets. It helps in revealing patterns and making cogent decisions based on aggregated information, rather than getting lost in individual data points. As you grow comfortable with grouping, you'll begin to appreciate how these capabilities can turn extensive, detailed datasets into meaningful, actionable insights. Through this structured approach, attain proficiency in not just handling data, but mastering it to steer your initiatives in the most informed directions.

ADVANCED PIVOT TABLE DATA FILTERING AND SLICING

You've mastered the art of constructing basic Pivot Tables and grouping data effectively. Now, let's steer towards refining your data analysis prowess with advanced filtering and slicing in Pivot Tables. These tools are not just about simplifying the data; they empower you to achieve a laser-focus on specific information, transforming sprawling data sets into targeted insights that can guide your most crucial business decisions.

Understanding Advanced Data Filtering

Imagine you are preparing an end-of-year performance report. Your dataset includes sales figures from multiple regions, product categories, and customer demographics spanning various dates. Yet, your task is to focus on the performance of a particular product line during the peak sale months. Here, advanced filtering capabilities of Pivot Tables allow you to display only the relevant slices of data, thereby tailoring the analysis to your specific needs.

1. **Using Date Filters**: Date filters are particularly useful in isolating data within specific time frames, such as quarters or fiscal periods. For this, you can use dynamic date filters like 'This Year', 'Last Month', 'Next Quarter', which automatically adjust to reflect the relevant periods as time progresses.

2. **Label and Value Filters**: These filters allow more granular control over what data appears in your Pivot Table. Label filters work by filtering data based on the labels in the Row or Column areas (say, showing only product categories that start with "Electro").

   Value filters come handy when you need to focus on metrics that meet certain criteria, such as sales exceeding a threshold or top 10 performing items.

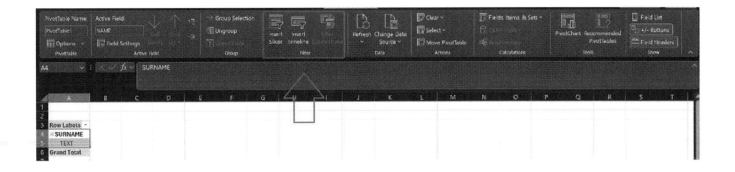

Exploring the Power of Slicers

While filters are great, slicers take data segmentation to a new level, providing a more intuitive and interactive way of on-the-fly filtering. They act like visual filters and can be connected to one or multiple Pivot Tables, creating a dashboard-like experience.

Create a slicer by selecting your Pivot Table, going to the PivotTable Analyze tab, and clicking on 'Insert Slicer'. Choose the fields which you frequently filter by, such as 'Region' or 'Product Type'. Once created, these slicers can be styled and arranged, enhancing your report's visual appeal and usability.

Deploying Timelines for Date Fields

Another powerful tool in your data analysis arsenal is the Timeline. It's exclusive to date fields and allows you to refine data based on time periods, visually. You insert a Timeline similarly to how you insert a slicer. Once added, you can slide across different time periods, watching your Pivot Table update instantaneously. This dynamic interaction provides a quick way to go from a yearly overview down to a day-by-day analysis.

Real-World Application: Sales Strategy Meeting

Let's contextualize this with a scenario. John, a sales manager, uses a Pivot Table to assess quarterly sales data. For an upcoming strategy meeting, he needs a crisp display of product performance segmented by region and only for the highest-selling products during the recent holiday season. John uses:

- **Multiple Slicers**: To dynamically filter the dashboard view between regions and product types.
- **Value Filters**: Set up to only display products that met the quarterly sales threshold.
- **Timelines**: Allowing a swift focus from quarterly data down to specific weeks of high retail traffic.

Now John doesn't just bring numbers to the strategy meeting; he brings tailored insights that can drive specific discussions on inventory planning and promotional strategies.

Tips for Efficient Filtering and Slicing

- **Consistency is key**: Make sure that the filters or slicers are necessary and relevant for the user. Avoid using too many filters which can lead the analysis to lose its focus.

- **Remember to refresh**: Just like with the raw Pivot Tables, any changes in the source data require a refresh so that filters and slicers accurately reflect the current data.
- **Organize for clarity**: Arrange slicers and timelines logically. Group related slicers together and use clear, concise naming for each to ensure they are self-explanatory.

Advanced filtering and slicing are not just about hiding or showing certain data; they are about augmenting your analytic capabilities in a way that you can interact with your data live, in meetings, or in reports, drilling down to the minutiae or zooming out for the bigger picture without ever losing sight of the context. Whether you're fine-tuning a sales presentation or exploring financial forecasts, these tools make sure that the data you need is always at your fingertips, rendered in the clearest and most actionable way. With practice, these sophisticated features of Pivot Tables will soon become part of your intuitive toolkit for smart data analysis.

INTEGRATING SUBTOTALS AND GRAND TOTALS

Navigating through the expansive territories of data in Excel can sometimes feel like overseeing a bustling marketplace, where each row and column bustle with activity and information. In such a scenario, summing up this activity—understanding the total sales or the aggregate scores—becomes imperative. This exact powerful summarization is what subtotals and grand totals in Pivot Tables help you achieve, transforming detailed data into comprehensible totals that tell the broader narrative of your data's story.

Understanding the Role of Subtotals and Grand Totals

In the world of data analysis, details are vital but so is the ability to zoom out to comprehend the bigger picture. Subtotals and grand totals serve this exact purpose. They provide a way to quickly view the summary data based on one or more categorical fields, helping you gauge overall performance or trends without flipping through individual data sheets.

When you activate subtotals in Pivot Tables, Excel automatically groups data according to the field you've chosen and then provides a summed figure for each group. Grand totals, on the other hand, take it up a notch by offering the total of all the data in your Pivot Table, serving as a comprehensive snapshot.

How to Integrate Subtotals

Imagine you're analyzing sales data where each transaction is detailed by product category and region. You'd want to know how each category is performing in each region and also gain an idea of the overall sales in each category.

1. **Insert Subtotals**: To insert subtotals, ensure your Pivot Table is set up with the categories you need (e.g., 'Region' and 'Product Category'). Right-click on an item within the row labels, navigate to 'Subtotal "Region"', and Excel will automatically insert a subtotal for each change in the region.

2. **Customizing Subtotals**: Not all subtotals have to be sums. Excel allows you to customize these to show averages, counts, max, min, and more. This customization can be accessed by clicking on the 'Value Field Settings' from the right-click menu and selecting the type of calculation you need under 'Summarize Value Field By'.

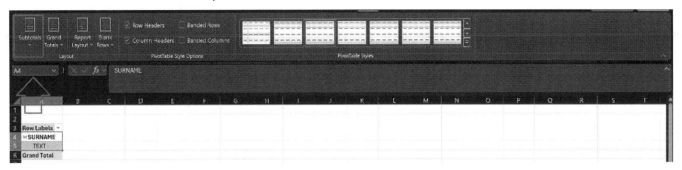

Incorporating Grand Totals

Grand totals are straightforward yet crucial, providing the sum total of all data across a Pivot Table.

- **Inserting Grand Totals**: By default, Pivot Tables include grand totals, but if not, you can easily turn them on by navigating to the 'Design' tab under PivotTable Tools, clicking on 'Grand Totals', and choosing 'On for Rows and Columns'.

- **Customizing Grand Totals**: For more refined control, you might only want a grand total for rows or perhaps just for columns, which is particularly useful in complex Pivot Tables with extensive data. The same menu allows selections like 'Off for Columns' or 'On for Rows Only', giving you the flexibility to set your table as needed.

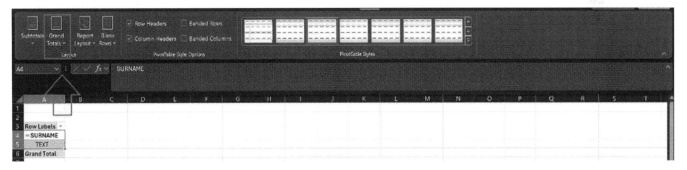

Streamlining Data Analysis with Clear Summaries

Subtotals and grand totals are not merely about finding the sum of numbers—they encapsulate the essence of your analysis, providing clear, actionable summaries that can guide business decisions. For instance, if quarterly sales targets are being evaluated, subtotals per month with a grand total at the end can immediately highlight performance trends and deviations.

Best Practices for Using Subtotals and Grand Totals

- **Clarity is Key**: Ensure that your table remains easy to read once subtotals are added. Overcrowding a Pivot Table with too many subtotals can lead to confusion rather than clarity.

- **Aligning with Objectives**: Align your subtotal and grand total placements with your analytical goals. Each subtotal should serve a purpose in the broader analysis scenario you are exploring.

- **Refresh to Update**: As data gets added or modified in your source sheets, ensure that you refresh your Pivot Tables to reflect updated subtotals and grand totals accurately.

Real-World Example: Educational Data Analysis

Consider a school administrator analyzing standardized test results by grade level across several classes. By setting up a Pivot Table to display scores by class with subtotals for each grade and a grand total at the end, the administrator could quickly identify which grades or classes might need additional resources or interventions based on their performance summaries.

In conclusion, subtotals and grand totals transform your Pivot Tables from detailed databases into powerful summary reports, each line telling part of a larger story. With these tools, you're equipped to bridge the gap between micro-level data inspection and macro-level strategic insights, ensuring that no significant trend or detail is overlooked in your analyses.

CHAPTER 7: EXCEL TECHNIQUES FOR EFFICIENCY

Stepping into Chapter 7, let's boost your journey through the marvels of Excel with a deep dive into efficiency-enhancing techniques. We previously laid the groundwork by introducing Excel's core tools and explored intermediate capabilities enhancing data presentation and analysis. Now, imagine yourself in the midst of a busy workday, flooded with tasks that require frequent and repetitive data handling. This scenario might seem daunting, but it's where Excel's true prowess comes to the rescue—where every second you save adds up to significant gains in your day.

In this portion of our guide, we'll explore how specific Excel techniques can streamline work processes, vastly reducing the time you spend on data management. Think of Excel not just as a tool for organizing data, but as your personal assistant, helping to automate the mundane, allowing you to focus on decisions and tasks that truly require your unique human touch.

We'll start by mastering advanced sorting methods. Imagine you have a spreadsheet with hundreds of entries. You need to view this data in multiple dimensions—perhaps sorting first by date, then by sales amount. Excel allows you to swiftly rearrange your data, helping to surface the most relevant information when you need it.

Next, the magic of Flash Fill will change the way you input data. Instead of manually typing out patterns repeatedly, Flash Fill recognizes patterns in your data input and completes it for you. This means less time typing, less chance for error, and more time for your core responsibilities.

Efficient data search and replacement as well as named ranges will also feature prominently here. With these capabilities, you'll learn to rapidly locate specific data within a sea of numbers and streamline your workflows by using named ranges to reference data across multiple worksheets.

By the end of this chapter, you will transform your workflow, turning complex tasks into simple, error-free operations. Our aim is not just to use Excel but to wield it in a way that multiplies your productivity, clearing the way for you to excel in your role. Think of this as not just learning—but empowering yourself with Excel.

COMPLEX SORTING METHODS: SORTING ON MULTIPLE LEVELS

Imagine you're analyzing a sales report with numerous entries scattered across various categories, regions, and time frames. The data feels like an unruly crowd, everyone jumbled together, making it nearly impossible to discern any meaningful patterns or insights. This is where Excel's ability to perform complex sorting on multiple levels becomes your strategic advantage, transforming chaos into order with just a few clicks.

Understanding Multi-Level Sorting

Complex sorting involves organizing data based on more than one criterion. For example, you might want to sort a sales report first by region, within each region by the sales manager, and within each manager's area by quarterly sales figures. This method brings a hierarchical structure to your data, enabling you to quickly navigate through layers of information and make informed decisions.

Step-by-Step: Implementing Multi-Level Sorting in Excel

Here's how you can apply multi-level sorting to an example data set: 1. **Prepare Your Data**: Ensure your data table is clear of blank rows and columns, as these can disrupt the sorting process. Excel's sorting functions work best when they're targeting contiguous cells grouped together as a dataset.

2. **Select Your Data**: Click and drag to highlight the cells you want to sort. If your data includes headers, make sure to include them in your selection. They play a key role in specifying the criteria for your sort.

3. **Access the Sort Dialog Box**: Navigate to the 'Data' tab on the Ribbon and click on 'Sort'. This opens a dialog box that provides options for adding multiple sorting levels.

4. **Adding Sort Levels**:

   o **First Level**: Choose the primary column you'd like to sort by from the 'Sort by' dropdown menu. Decide whether you want to sort in ascending or descending order.

   o **Add Level**: Click on 'Add Level' to introduce additional criteria. For each level, select the column you want to sort next and specify the order.

   o Repeat this step until all your sorting criteria are lined up. You can move levels up or down to prioritize how Excel applies the sorting.

5. **Refining the Sort Process**: If your data involves text, you can customize how Excel handles the capitalization by using the 'Options' button in the sort dialog box. For numbers, you might decide whether to treat them as numbers or text, especially useful when dealing with alphanumeric data.

6. **Finalize and Apply**: Once you've arranged your sorting layers and defined their behavior, click 'OK' in the sort dialog box. Excel will process your commands and reorder your dataset as specified.

Practical Tips for Effective Sorting

- **Consistency in Data Entry**: For sorting to work flawlessly, your data must be consistently formatted. Ensure that all entries in a specific column are of the same data type (e.g., all text or all numbers).

- **Backup Your Data**: Before you perform any major data manipulation, including sorting, always make a backup of your dataset. Sorting can be undone using the undo feature, but having a backup is a safety net you shouldn't ignore.

- **Use Tables**: Convert your data range into a table (Insert -> Table). Tables offer enhanced sorting options and automatically exclude any total rows from the sort to avoid mixing summary data with detailed entries.

Applying Sorts to Real-world Data

Consider you are tasked with analyzing annual customer feedback data to identify trends in satisfaction across multiple service centers. Each record logs the customer's location, service center, agent ID, the date of interaction, and satisfaction rating. By using multi-level sorting, you can first view the data by location, within each location by service center, and then by agent ID in ascending order of date. This drill-down method allows you to effectively compare agents' performance over time within their specific environments.

Multi-level sorting in Excel isn't just about organizing rows; it's about unlocking the narrative layered within your data. With the skills developed in this chapter, you'll be able to not only find the story your data tells but also present it in a structured, understandable manner that informs strategic business decisions. Whether it's preparing a presentation for key stakeholders or conducting a thorough data analysis, mastering complex sorting methods ensures that you always bring clarity and precision to the table, enhancing both your efficiency and your credibility as a data handler.

AUTOMATING DATA ENTRY WITH FLASH FILL

In the world of Excel, one of the most gratifying features is its ability to simplify and automate tedious data entry tasks, giving you more time to focus on complex analyses or creative solutions to business challenges. One such feature that exemplifies this capability is Flash Fill, a tool designed to make pattern recognition and data entry not only easier but virtually instantaneous.

Understanding Flash Fill

Introduced in more recent versions of Excel, Flash Fill is a smart tool that automatically fills in data when it recognizes a pattern in your actions. It is particularly useful in situations where data needs to be formatted or extracted based on a consistent rule or pattern, such as splitting full names into first and last names or combining date fields into a single uniform format.

How Flash Fill Works

Let's say you have a column of full names, and you need to extract just the first name in an adjacent column. Traditionally, you might use text functions or a complex formula. However, with Flash Fill, you simply start typing the first names based on the data in the first column and Excel immediately recognizes the pattern and offers to fill in the rest of the names for you.

Utilizing Flash Fill Effectively

1. **Initiate Flash Fill:**
   o Start by entering your desired result in a cell adjacent to the dataset you're working with. For example, if you're extracting first names from a list of full names, type the first name corresponding to the first cell in the list.
   o Press Enter to move to the next cell and start to type the next corresponding entry. As soon as Excel detects a pattern, it will show a grayed-out preview of what it can fill for the rest of the column.
   o Simply press Enter once more, and Excel will carry out the Flash Fill, populating the column with the extracted data.

2. **Manual Triggering:**
   o If Excel doesn't automatically suggest a Flash Fill, you can trigger it manually by selecting the cell where you began the pattern, then go to Data in the Ribbon and click on Flash Fill. Alternatively, you can use the keyboard shortcut Ctrl + E.

3. **Correcting and Refining:**
   o If the Flash Fill results aren't perfect, this often points to inconsistencies in the provided data or in the initial examples you provided. Verify the consistency of your pattern inputs, adjust as necessary, and try again.
   o For more complex patterns, providing a few more examples before triggering Flash Fill can help the system better understand the intended pattern.

Practical Applications of Flash Fill

Imagine you're organizing a large list of client information where the clients' names, phone numbers, and email addresses are all in a single column, but you need them separated for a mailing campaign. Manually parsing these can be time-consuming and prone to errors. With Flash Fill, you can automate the separation by simply providing a couple of examples for each type of data you need to extract. This not only accelerates the process but reduces the likelihood of mistyping or misplacing information.

Flash Fill is not limited to text data—it can be used creatively with numerical data as well, such as reformatting dates, extracting area codes from phone numbers, or even creating new numerical identifiers based on existing data.

Best Practices When Using Flash Fill

- **Keep Data Clean**: Flash Fill works best with well-organized and cleanly formatted data. Before employing Flash Fill, ensure there are no extra spaces or inconsistencies in your data.
- **Provide Clear Patterns**: The accuracy of Flash Fill depends significantly on the examples you provide. The clearer and more consistent your examples, the better Flash Fill can perform.
- **Use Wisely**: While Flash Fill is powerful, it's not always the best tool for every job, especially when working with extremely large datasets or when data does not follow a discernible pattern. In such cases, more sophisticated formulas or scripts might be necessary.

Real-World Example for Illustration

Consider a sales report containing a column with transaction codes that state the product type, date, and transaction number all jumbled together. The task is to extract just the transaction number. By illustrating how to use Flash Fill to simplify this task, the productivity gains become evident, allowing more time to focus on analyzing transaction trends rather than data entry chores.

In conclusion, Flash Fill exemplifies Excel's capability to enhance productivity through automation. It's a simple yet effective tool that, when used correctly, can significantly reduce the manual workload associated with data entry and adjustment tasks. By integrating this powerful feature into your daily Excel use, you transform not just your workflow but also unlock new levels of efficiency in your data management tasks.

EFFECTIVE DATA SEARCH AND REPLACEMENT

In the bustling world of modern business, where data drives decisions and timely information is gold, the ability to swiftly locate and update data in Excel can be a game-changer for productivity. Whether correcting an erroneous entry, updating information, or compiling reports, mastering effective search and replacement techniques in Excel will not only save you time but also ensure accuracy and consistency across your documents.

Exploring Excel's Find and Replace Function

At the heart of effective data manipulation in Excel lies the 'Find and Replace' feature—a powerful tool designed to help you quickly locate and modify specific data across large spreadsheets. This feature is not merely about correcting misspellings or updating names; it's about transforming how you manage and interact with your data.

How to Effectively Use Find and Replace

1. **Launching Find and Replace**: Open the 'Find and Replace' dialog box by pressing Ctrl + F for Find or Ctrl + H for Replace. This window offers various options to refine your search and replacement actions.

2. **Configuring Your Search**:
   o In the 'Find what' box, enter the text, number, or phrase you are searching for.
   o Use the 'Replace with' box if you intend to replace the found values. Here, you can enter the new data that should replace the old.

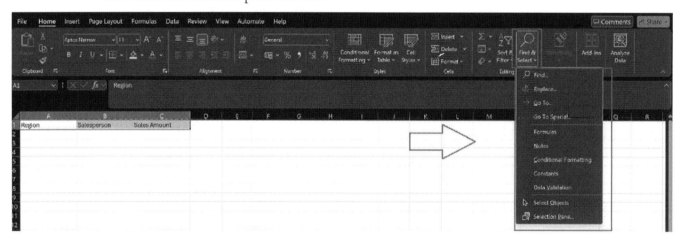

3. **Setting Search Options**:
   o You can expand the dialog box by selecting "Options>>" to reveal additional settings. These allow you to search within formulas, values, or comments, fitting various data interrogation needs.

o Define the scope of your search, whether within a specific worksheet or the entire workbook. You can also decide whether to look in rows or columns, which is particularly useful in large datasets.

4. **Executing and Reviewing Results**:

   o After setting your parameters, click 'Find Next' to locate the first occurrence or 'Find All' for a list of all occurrences. For replacements, clicking 'Replace' will substitute the current occurrence, while 'Replace All' will change every match in the document.

   o Review each replacement to ensure accuracy, particularly when making widespread changes, to avoid unintended modifications.

Practical Examples and Applications

Consider you're preparing financial statements and realize a recurring expense account was misnamed throughout an extensive spreadsheet. Using 'Find and Replace,' you can quickly correct every instance, ensuring your documents reflect the correct information without manually searching through potentially thousands of entries.

For marketing professionals, updating product names or codes in promotional plans can be streamlined using this feature. Instead of manually locating each occurrence, 'Find and Replace' automates the process, significantly reducing the time spent on such tasks.

Advanced Tips for Using Find and Replace

- **Using Wildcards**: For more complex searches, Excel supports wildcard characters such as the asterisk (*) and question mark (?). An asterisk replaces any series of characters, and a question mark replaces a single character. This is particularly useful when dealing with data that has slight variations in its naming conventions.

- **Search Formats**: Sometimes, the difference isn't in the text but in the formatting. Excel allows you to search for specific data formats, enabling you to find and modify data points based on their visual appearance, such as font type, color, or cell background.

- **Case Sensitivity**: By default, 'Find and Replace' is not case-sensitive. However, you can make it so by adjusting options, allowing for precise data management aligned with the needs of sensitive datasets.

More Than Just a Tool—A Strategy

Employing 'Find and Replace' effectively in Excel isn't only about knowing which buttons to press. It's about understanding the data landscape of your spreadsheets, anticipating where errors might occur, and proactively managing the data to support decision-making processes. It turns a simple feature into a critical strategy for maintaining the integrity and usefulness of your data.

Integration into Daily Operations

Integrating sophisticated search and replace tactics into your regular Excel use not only boosts efficiency but also ensures a higher level of data accuracy. Imagine compiling end-of-year reports or preparing datasets for important meetings; knowing you can rely on Excel to help manage and rectify data quickly allows you to approach these tasks with confidence.

Effective data search and replacement in Excel bridges the gap between raw data management and strategic information handling. By mastering these techniques, you elevate your role from a data entry personnel to a strategic data overseer, enabling you to manage spreadsheets with precision and foresight.

This capability is not just about making corrections; it's about owning the process of data management and becoming a pivotal part of your team's success in handling information efficiently.

ESTABLISHING NAMED RANGES FOR ENHANCED FORMULA MANAGEMENT

Navigating through large datasets or complex formulas in Excel can often feel like a daunting quest where ease and efficiency seem out of reach. However, Excel offers a powerful feature that serves as a navigational beacon, guiding you through these intricate data seas with increased precision and ease: Named Ranges. By defining named ranges, you not only enhance the readability and manageability of your formulas but also significantly streamline your workflow, making it more intuitive and less error-prone.

Understanding Named Ranges

Named Ranges allow you to assign a memorable name to a cell or range of cells. Instead of remembering or referencing obscure cell addresses in your formulas, you can use these names, which act like clearly marked signposts, helping you and others understand what the data represents at a glance.

How to Create Named Ranges

1. **Select the Range**: Begin by selecting the cell or group of cells you want to name. This could be a single cell that holds a critical value (like a sales tax rate) or a range that you frequently use in your calculations (such as a column of monthly sales figures).

2. **Define the Name**: With your cells selected, go to the Formulas tab, click on 'Define Name', and enter a name in the Name field. Excel names must start with a letter or underscore and cannot include spaces (use underscores or camelCase for multi-word names).

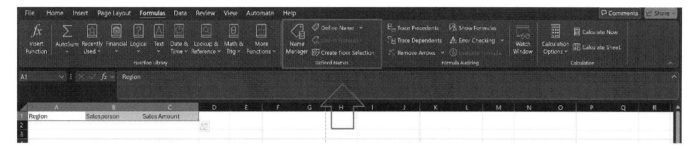

3. **Apply and Use the Named Range**: Once you have defined a named range, you can start using it in formulas anywhere in your workbook. For example, instead of typing =SUM(B2:B10), you could name B2:B10 as "MonthlySales" and simply write =SUM(MonthlySales). This makes your formulas much easier to read and understand.

Benefits of Using Named Ranges

- **Clarity and Simplicity**: Using named ranges clarifies what your formulas are doing, turning cryptic cell references into meaningful descriptions.

- **Ease of Maintenance**: Updating data becomes easier with named ranges. If you need to expand the "MonthlySales" range, you can simply update the range definition without having to modify every formula that references it.

- **Reduced Errors**: By eliminating the need to repeatedly input cell references, named ranges reduce the likelihood of errors in formula creation, particularly in large and complex spreadsheets.

Practical Applications of Named Ranges

A financial analyst could use named ranges to track quarterly earnings reports more efficiently. By assigning the name "Q1Earnings" to the range containing the first quarter's data, the analyst can easily refer to this data in complex financial models without constantly scrolling through the spreadsheet to ensure the correct cell range is used in calculations.

Advanced Techniques: Dynamic Named Ranges

For those who deal with data that changes in size, such as a list that receives new entries regularly, dynamic named ranges can be particularly beneficial. These ranges adjust automatically as you add or remove data.

- **Creating a Dynamic Named Range**: Use the OFFSET function in the name definition to make a range grow or shrink dynamically. For example, defining a name with =OFFSET($A$1,0,0,COUNTA($A:$A),1) creates a range starting from A1 that expands downward as new items are added to column A.

Integrating Named Ranges into Daily Workflows

Implementing named ranges in your daily Excel tasks can elevate your productivity significantly. Imagine preparing a monthly performance report that involves numerous data sources and complex calculations. By establishing named ranges for each data segment and key metric, you can build your report not only with greater speed but also with increased accuracy, ensuring that all stakeholders receive clear and precise information.

Incorporating named ranges into your Excel practice transforms your approach from simply tackling data to strategically managing it. It's akin to upgrading from paper maps to GPS in navigation: by marking critical data points with clear and consistent signposts, you pave the way for smoother journeys through your spreadsheets. Whether you're a seasoned data analyst or a finance professional, mastering named ranges will provide you with a tool that enhances both the sophistication and simplicity of your data management tasks.

CHAPTER 8: ESSENTIAL DAILY FUNCTIONS

Welcome to Chapter 8: Essential Daily Functions, where we delve into the tools and functions that can transform your everyday Excel tasks from tedious to triumphant. Imagine starting your workday with certainty, knowing that the spreadsheet before you—a tool that once seemed so daunting—is now an open book of opportunities. That's what we're aiming for in this chapter.

Here, we explore essential daily functions that will not only make your data manipulations easier but will also boost your confidence as you breeze through tasks that used to eat up your precious time. We'll start with logical operations such as IF, AND, OR, which are the backbone of decision-making within Excel. Understanding these functions allows you to automate decision-making on your sheets, letting Excel do the heavy lifting whether it's determining budget approvals or project statuses.

Next, we step into the world of text manipulation with functions like CONCATENATE, LEFT, RIGHT, and MID. These functions are not just about pulling characters together or apart—they reshape how your data looks and feels, making it more readable and approachable. Whether you're summarizing data or preparing it for a presentation, mastering these functions means you can handle text in Excel as deftly as any word processor.

We'll then dive into data retrieval functions, including the venerable VLOOKUP and its sibling HLOOKUP. These functions are often viewed with a mix of necessity and apprehension. However, with our step-by-step approach, you'll see how these tools can swiftly become your best friends in navigating vast tables of data, linking different datasets with a simplicity that feels like magic.

Finally, we'll cover the fundamental date and time functions. These are your keys to managing timelines, deadlines, and historical data. Understanding how to manipulate and calculate dates and times in Excel will save you not just minutes but hours—perhaps even days across the span of your career.

Each part of this chapter builds on what you've learned before but also sets the stage for more complex applications. By breaking down these functions with practical examples and actionable tips, we aim to equip you with a robust toolkit that makes Excel feel less like a software program and more like a natural extension of your thought process. Let's reduce the stress and increase the joy of working with data, together.

LOGICAL OPERATIONS: IF, AND, OR

Understanding and using logical operations in Excel can significantly enhance your ability to make decisions and analyze data on your spreadsheets. Logical functions like IF, AND, and OR are powerful tools that help you sort through, classify, and respond to a diverse array of data variables. Let's explore each of these functions in detail, focusing on simple steps and practical examples that bring these concepts to life.

The IF Function

The IF function is one of the most frequently used logical functions in Excel. It is incredibly versatile and allows you to perform conditional checks on your data. The basic syntax for an IF statement is:

=IF(condition, value_if_true, value_if_false)

Let's relate this to a real-world example: Imagine you're managing a team's project deadlines. You need to determine if tasks are on schedule. If a task is on schedule, the cell should show "On Track"; if it's overdue, it should show "Behind".

Here's how you could write this function:

=IF(A1 > TODAY(), "On Track", "Behind")

In this formula, A1 contains the due date of the project. If the date in A1 is greater than today's date (TODAY()), Excel returns "On Track"; otherwise, it returns "Behind".

Combining Multiple Conditions with AND

The AND function becomes useful when you want to test multiple conditions simultaneously. It returns TRUE if all the conditions are true, and FALSE if any one of the conditions is false.

Looking at our project management scenario, suppose you now want to check if a task is on track based on two criteria: the due date and whether the task is at least 75% complete. Here's how you might use the AND function:

=IF(AND(A1 > TODAY(), B1 >= 75%), "On Track", "Behind")

In this case, A1 contains the due date and B1 the completion percentage. This formula checks if the due date is still in the future and the task is at least 75% complete. If both conditions are met, it returns "On Track"; otherwise, "Behind".

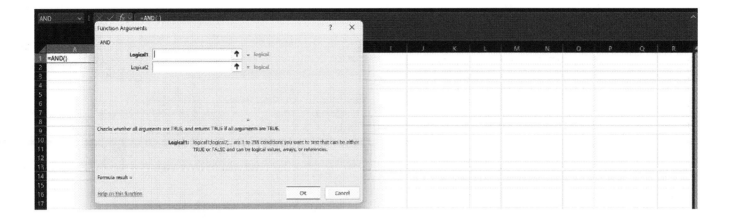

Incorporating Flexibility with the OR Function

Now, suppose you want to provide some leeway on the task completion. You decide a task can also be considered "On Track" if the completion is below 75% but the task isn't due for another 30 days. The OR function allows you to add this flexibility. OR returns TRUE if any of the given conditions are true.

Here's how the OR function can be integrated:

=IF(OR(A1 > TODAY(), AND(A1 >= TODAY() + 30, B1 >= 50%)), "On Track", "Behind")

Here, A1 is still the due date, and B1 is the completion percentage. This function now checks whether the due date is still in the future or if the task is at least 50% complete and due no sooner than 30 days. This gives your team extra time to complete tasks that are not immediately due.

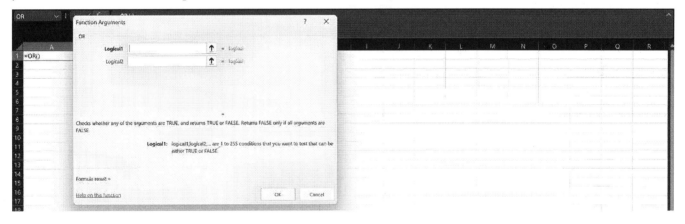

Practical Excel Function Tips:

- **Use Named Ranges**: To make your formulas easier to read and manage, use named ranges for your conditions. For example, instead of using cell references like A1 or B1 in your formulas, define names for these cells (like DueDate and Completion).

- **Document Your Formulas**: Always add comments next to your complex formulas explaining what they accomplish. This makes it easier for others to understand your work or for you to remember when you review your spreadsheet weeks or months later.

Real-World Applications

Consider how these functions apply in different scenarios—beyond project management. For instance, in a school setting, you could use an IF function to automatically determine student grade outcomes (=IF(C1>=90, "A", "B")). In human resources, AND could be used to assess eligibility for a bonus (=IF(AND(C1>=10000, D1>=90%), "Eligible for Bonus", "Not Eligible")).

By mastering these logical functions, you empower yourself to make smarter, faster decisions with your data. Remember, the goal isn't just to function effectively—it's to excel. These tools are more than simple functions; they are the gateway to sophisticated data analysis and decision-making that can elevate your professional capabilities and your confidence in using Excel.

TEXT MANIPULATION FUNCTIONS: CONCATENATE, LEFT, RIGHT, MID

Mastering text manipulation functions in Excel such as CONCATENATE, LEFT, RIGHT, and MID can open up a myriad of possibilities for organizing and presenting your data more effectively. These functions allow you to tailor text data to fit the needs of your analysis or presentation, ensuring that your spreadsheets are not only functional but also clear and informative.

CONCATENATE: Merging Text Seamlessly

The CONCATENATE function is straightforward: it combines two or more text strings into one string. The beauty of CONCATENATE lies in its ability to bring together information from different parts of your spreadsheet in a readable format. For instance, if you have a list of first names in one column and last names in another, CONCATENATE helps you easily combine these into full names.

Suppose you have the first names in column A and the last names in column B. Here's how you could use CONCATENATE to merge these names in column C:

=CONCATENATE(A1, " ", B1)

This formula adds a space (" ") between the first name and the last name, ensuring that the combined name reads correctly as "John Doe" rather than "JohnDoe".

LEFT, RIGHT, and MID: Extracting Substrings

Often, you need to pull out specific parts of a text string. Maybe you're only interested in the first few letters of a string, or perhaps you need to extract a substring from the middle. This is where the LEFT, RIGHT, and MID functions come into play.

- **LEFT**: This function extracts a specified number of characters from the beginning of a text string. For example, if you want to extract the first three letters of a list of strings in column A, you would use:

    =LEFT(A1, 3)

This might be used to get a quick abbreviation of the names or to extract area codes from phone numbers.

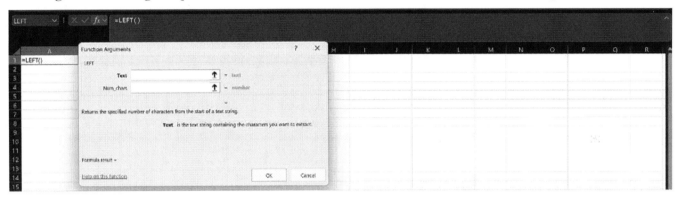

- **RIGHT**: Opposite to LEFT, this function extracts from the end of a string. To get the last four digits of a string in column A (useful for retrieving the last few characters of an account number or similar data), you might use:

    =RIGHT(A1, 4)

- **MID**: MID is useful when you need to extract a substring from the middle of a text string. This function requires three arguments — the text string, the start position, and the number of characters to extract. For instance, to extract three characters starting from the second character:

    =MID(A1, 2, 3)

Practical Excel Function Tips

- **Combining Text Functions**: You can combine these text functions to solve more complex problems. For example, suppose you want to create a standardized identifier that involves using part of a surname and part of a date. You could use a combination of text functions to assemble this identifier in the format you require.

- **Dynamic Text Adjustments**: Adjust the number of characters you extract based on specific conditions using IF statements along with text functions. This can be particularly useful in data cleanup tasks.

Real-World Applications

Imagine you work in HR and receive a spreadsheet containing full names, but your task is to send out mail-merged emails, which require first names only. A simple use of the LEFT or MID function could help you automate the extraction of first names, depending on the structure of the names in your data.

Or, consider a scenario in customer service where ticket numbers are generated as a combination of date, time, and an unique identifier. Using text manipulation functions can help you swiftly dissect these ticket numbers into their component parts for further analysis.

These functions are not merely academic; they are tools that, once mastered, can markedly increase both the speed and quality of your work. The efficiency gains from knowing when and how to use them can significantly reduce the hours spent on mundane data manipulation tasks, giving you more time to focus on analysis and decision-making.

In conclusion, becoming proficient with Excel's text manipulation functions empowers you to handle a wide array of tasks involving text, from simple tweaks that align with your presentation style to complex data processing jobs. These skills are essential for anyone looking to enhance their capability to manage and present data effectively in Excel.

DATA RETRIEVAL FUNCTIONS: VLOOKUP, HLOOKUP

In the realm of Excel, understanding and effectively using data retrieval functions like VLOOKUP and HLOOKUP translate directly into enhanced proficiency and swiftness with your spreadsheets. These functions are essential for anyone who often works with extensive datasets and needs a straightforward way to retrieve specific information without manually searching through columns or rows. Let's explore these functions in a context that vividly illustrates their utility and execution.

VLOOKUP: Vertical Lookup

VLOOKUP stands for Vertical Lookup. It is tailored for searching down a column for a key and returning a value from a specified cell in the same row. Here's a relatable example: imagine you are managing a customer database, and you need to find specific client information without scrolling through hundreds of entries.

The syntax for VLOOKUP is:

$$=VLOOKUP(lookup\_value, table\_array, col\_index\_num, [range\_lookup])$$

- **lookup_value**: This is what you want to find. This might be a client ID or name.
- **table_array**: The range of columns where Excel should search. This includes the data you want to find as well as the data you want to retrieve.
- **col*index*num**: After finding the row with the lookup value, this number tells Excel which column to pull from that row.
- **range_lookup**: This tells Excel whether you want an exact match (use FALSE) or an approximate match (use TRUE).

For a concrete scenario, suppose you have a client ID, and you need to quickly find their phone number. You have the client ID in cell A1, the client IDs in column B, and their corresponding phone numbers in column C. Your formula would be:

$$=VLOOKUP(A1, B:C, 2, FALSE)$$

This formula checks the B column for the client ID you specified in A1 and retrieves the phone number from the C column of the matching row.

HLOOKUP: Horizontal Lookup

In contrast, HLOOKUP, or Horizontal Lookup, is used to search a row and then return a value from a column you specify, based on the row number. It's useful when your data table is set up horizontally.

The HLOOKUP formula goes like this:

=HLOOKUP(lookup_value, table_array, row_index_num, [range_lookup])

- **lookup_value**: What you're looking for horizontally across the top of your spreadsheet.
- **table** *array*: *The range where Excel will look for the lookup* value and the data to retrieve.
- **row** *index* **num**: After finding the column with the lookup value, this number tells Excel which row to pull from.
- **range_lookup**: Like in VLOOKUP, this determines whether you seek an exact or approximate match.

Consider you are analyzing a product database where each product's initial stock count from January to December is listed in the first row, and you need to report the stock count for May. You could set up your HLOOKUP like so:

=HLOOKUP("May", A1:M13, 13, FALSE)

This searches for "May" across the top row A1 to M1, and returns the value from the 13th row in the same column, allowing you to dynamically pull data across horizontally arranged tables.

Practical Excel Function Tips

- **Alignment**: Always ensure your data is appropriately aligned vertically for VLOOKUP and horizontally for HLOOKUP to avoid data retrieval errors.
- **Data Formatting**: Confirm that the data format in your lookup *value matches the format of the data in your table* array to ensure accurate results.

Leveraging VLOOKUP and HLOOKUP in Real-World Scenarios

In a business setting, these functions are incredible time-savers. For example, a sales manager could use VLOOKUP to cross-reference invoice numbers with customer names to generate personalized follow-up emails efficiently. Health professionals might utilize HLOOKUP in patient databases where horizontal fields include various test results, and quick retrieval is necessary for comparison and diagnosis during patient consultations.

Mastering VLOOKUP and HLOOKUP not only streamlines interactions with your data but also significantly reduces the probability of human error. As you become familiar with these functions, you'll find that they help to simplify what might initially seem like daunting tasks, transforming them into routine data manipulations that can be performed with both speed and accuracy.

FUNDAMENTAL DATE AND TIME FUNCTIONS CHAPTER

In the tapestry of Excel features, date and time functions hold a vivid thread, giving life to columns filled with numbers that represent moments. Understanding how to manipulate these figures is crucial for anyone needing to track hours worked, calculate deadlines, or manage any event that is time-sensitive. Let's dive into the fundamental date and time functions in Excel, illustrating them through scenarios you likely encounter in your data-driven adventures.

Excel contains several built-in functions for managing dates and times, each designed to help you convert, extract, and compute dates and times swiftly. We'll explore some of the most frequently used functions—TODAY, NOW, DATE, YEAR, MONTH, DAY, and NETWORKDAYS—cementing our understanding with examples that illuminate their practical applications.

TODAY: Capturing Current Date

The TODAY function is incredibly straightforward; it requires no arguments and simply returns the current date:

=TODAY()

This function is dynamically updated each time the worksheet recalculates. For instance, if you are tracking a deadline, you can calculate the days remaining until the deadline by subtracting TODAY from the future date:

=DeadlineDate - TODAY()

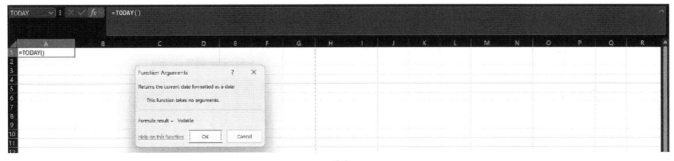

NOW: Current Date and Time

Like TODAY, the NOW function needs no arguments and provides the current date and time:

=NOW()

NOW is ideal when you need a timestamp in your data logging, perhaps marking when data entries were recorded or updated.

DATE: Creating a Specific Date

The DATE function allows you to construct a date from individual year, month, and day components:

=DATE(year, month, day)

A practical use of the DATE function might be to generate a series of end-of-month review dates. For instance, if you start with a known date and need to find the same day in the next month:

=DATE(YEAR(A1), MONTH(A1) + 1, DAY(A1))

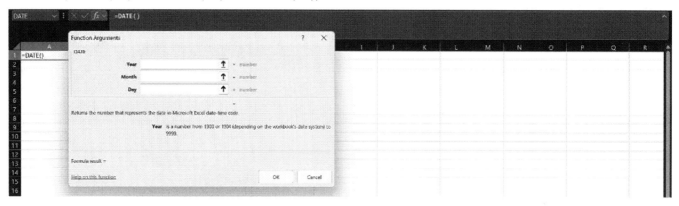

YEAR, MONTH, DAY: Extracting Date Components

These companion functions cleanly extract the year, month, and day from a date, which can be particularly useful in data analysis and reporting:

=YEAR(serial_number)

=MONTH(serial_number)

=DAY(serial_number)

For example, if you have a column of dates and need to analyze how many events happened in a particular year, you could extract the year from each date and summarize the data based on these years.

NETWORKDAYS: Calculating Workdays

When planning projects, calculating the actual number of working days between dates—omitting weekends and holidays—is vital:

=NETWORKDAYS(start_date, end_date, [holidays])

By defining a holiday range, you can refine your workdays' count, ensuring accurate timelines and resource planning.

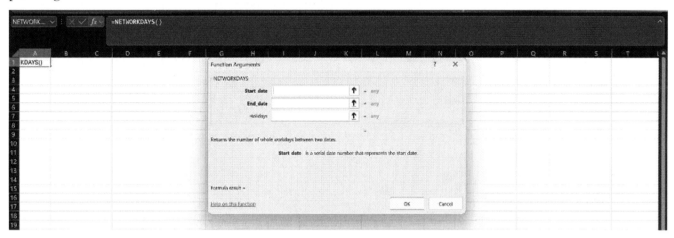

Applying Date and Time Functions in Real-World Scenarios

Consider a project manager who needs to track the duration of tasks. By employing a mix of date functions like DATE, NETWORKDAYS, and NOW, the manager can create a dashboard that dynamically reports on project status, calculating outstanding days and highlighting overdue tasks.

For human resources professionals, combining NETWORKDAYS with TODAY helps in figuring out the number of workdays left before an employee's evaluation or contract renewal, facilitating better planning and timely decision-making.

Practical Excel Function Tips

- **Precision**: Ensure that date calculations in Excel consider the correct start or end date, especially when dealing with inclusive versus exclusive ranges.
- **Formatting**: Always ensure your cells are appropriately formatted for dates or times to prevent confusion and errors in your calculations.

In essence, mastering Excel's date and time functions not only streamlines your interactions with date-based data but also enhances your ability to conduct timely analysis, project management, and planning. Whether you're scheduling events, analyzing trends over time, or planning projects, these functions are indispensable tools in your Excel toolkit, empowering you to manage time with precision and clarity.

CHAPTER 9: FUNDAMENTALS OF CHARTING WITH EXCEL

Imagine you're presenting a major project at work. As you walk your team through the complex data, you unveil a series of clear, compelling charts. Instantly, the room lights up with understanding. This is the power of mastering Excel charting—a fundamental tool that transforms raw data into insightful visual stories.

In Excel, charts are not just tools; they are the bridge between data complexity and strategic clarity. Whether you're aiming to visually summarize sales trends, operational efficiencies, or financial forecasts, charts become your go-to method for impactful data presentation.

Chapter 9, "Fundamentals of Charting with Excel," is designed to equip you with the skills to create and customize charts that not only look professional but also serve a strategic purpose. We begin by selecting the right chart types—understanding that the nature of your data determines the chart you use. A pie chart might be perfect for showing market share distribution, while a line chart could best illustrate sales trends over time.

We will then dive into the nuts and bolts of chart creation. You'll learn how to insert a chart and how to manipulate its design to suit your specific needs. Customization is key in making your charts speak clearly and effectively. We'll explore how to modify colors, adjust labels, and add elements like trendlines or data labels, enhancing not just aesthetics but also readability and comprehension.

Moreover, we'll tackle common challenges like overcrowded visuals and confusing layouts, providing practical tips on how to streamline your charts for maximum impact. By the end of this chapter, you'll be adept at using Excel's charting tools not just to display data, but to tell a compelling story with it.

Through real-world examples, you'll see how different industries leverage Excel charts, giving you a broad perspective on how these skills apply across various scenarios. By chapter's end, you'll feel confident about integrating these charting fundamentals into your daily work, ready to turn complex data into clear, persuasive visuals that can inform decisions and drive business strategies.

SELECTING APPROPRIATE CHART TYPES FOR DATA

In the world of Excel, selecting the right chart for your data is much like choosing the right tool for a job—it can make the difference between further confusion and crystal-clear understanding. The beauty of data visualization through charts lies in their ability to turn complex data sets into accessible visual insights. Understanding the various chart types and when to use them can tremendously elevate your ability to communicate effectively.

When you embark on the journey of creating a chart in Excel, the first step is always to consider the story your data is telling. Each chart type has a unique way of illuminating patterns, trends, and comparisons in data, and the choice of chart can either clarify or cloud the conveyed message.

Bar Charts and Column Charts Let's consider a scenario where you want to compare the sales performance of different products over a quarter. Bar charts and column charts shine in such comparisons, portraying data through rectangular bars, where the length of the bar corresponds to the data value. The choice between a bar and a column chart can be as simple as the layout: bars spread horizontally while columns stand vertically. This small orientation difference can be chosen based on space constraints or aesthetic considerations.

Line Charts Moving to trend analysis, imagine you are tracking the growth of sales over several months or evaluating traffic trends on a website. Line charts are perfect for viewing such continuous data over time, connecting data points with a continuous line. This makes it easy to identify trends, such as increases or seasonal declines, providing a simple and clear view of the ups and downs through time.

Pie Charts For showing proportions, pie charts offer a visually engaging way to depict how parts of a whole are distributed. For example, if you're analyzing market share or the percentage distribution of expenses across different departments, a pie chart makes these proportions easy to digest at a glance. However, it's advised to keep the number of segments low, as too many slices can complicate the clarity of the presentation.

Scatter Plots When you delve into examining relationships between two variables, scatter plots become exceptionally useful. Suppose a business wants to analyze the relationship between advertising spend and revenue gain. By plotting these two variables, scatter plots can help reveal correlations—whether positive, negative, or nonexistent—thus aiding in predictive analysis and strategic planning.

Pivot Charts Derived from PivotTables, pivot charts excel at handling multifaceted data in dynamic ways. If you need to quickly switch between different data views or drill down into specifics, a pivot chart adjusts interactively, allowing for a nuanced exploration of the data.

Combination Charts At times, a single type of chart might not suffice to express the complexity of the data effectively. Combination charts that use different chart types—for instance, combining a column and a line chart—can illustrate multiple types of data simultaneously. This dual approach can be particularly effective in scenarios where you need to compare a set of values while also showing a cumulative total, such as monthly revenue aligned against total profit over a year.

Practical Tips for Chart Selection 1. **Understand Your Data**: Before you choose a chart, deeply analyze what your data entails and what you want to communicate. This understanding is crucial in selecting the most effective visual representation. 2. **Keep It Simple**: Opt for a chart type that conveys the message in the simplest form. Overcomplicating a visual can detract from the data's message. 3. **Consider Your Audience**: Tailor your chart to the familiarity and expectations of your audience. What works in an academic report might not suit a business meeting.

Examples in Action Consider Jane, an entrepreneur who uses Excel to keep track of her startup's finances. By using combination charts, she presents her monthly expenses and income streams side-by-side, which not only simplifies her financial review meetings but clarifies decision-making processes regarding budget adjustments.

In another instance, a healthcare administrator uses line charts to track patient admissions over the year. This visualization helps the hospital management easily spot trends and prepare better for upcoming busy periods by adjusting staff and resource allocation.

Understanding and mastering the selection of appropriate chart types fundamentally changes how you interact with data. It shifts Excel from being just a tool for number crunching to a powerful storytelling device, capable of presenting data in the most insightful and impactful manner. As you continue to explore these chart types in Excel, remember that every choice in charting is a step towards better data understanding and communication.

CHART CREATION AND CUSTOMIZATION

Creating and customizing charts in Excel is like painting on a canvas, except your paints are data, and your brushes are Excel's tools. This process not only involves the technical steps of incorporating a chart but also the art of making sure it tells your data's story as clearly and effectively as possible. Let's walk through these steps, understanding how each part of the chart can be modified to better suit your needs, making your data not just visible but truly insightful.

Starting with Chart Creation

The first step in Excel charting is selecting your data. This is crucial because the accuracy of what you display depends on the correctness of the data selected. Once your data is highlighted, inserting a chart is straightforward. Head to the 'Insert' tab and choose the chart type that best fits your data narrative. Excel offers a range of charts including column, bar, line, pie, and more. By clicking on your preferred chart, Excel generates a basic version using your selected data.

Customizing the Chart Area

After insertion, your chart might look too generic or not quite fit for presentation. This is where customization plays a role. Starting with resizing and moving your chart provides a basic foundation for the visual aspect of your presentation. Clicking on the chart will show 'Chart Tools' in the toolbar, under which you find options like 'Design' and 'Format'. These tools allow you to adjust the layout and style of your chart.

Tweaking Chart Elements

Most charts comprise several key elements—title, axis labels, legends, and data series. Each element can be added, removed, or customized by navigating to the 'Chart Elements' button (a plus sign next to the chart). Here, you can decide to show or hide things like axis titles or data labels and even decide their position relative to the chart.

Imagine you are preparing a presentation for the quarterly sales report. Adding a clearly readable title and axis descriptions can immediately make your chart more informative. For instance, rather than a generic "Sales Over Time," a title like "Q1 Sales Performance by Product Line" provides immediate context.

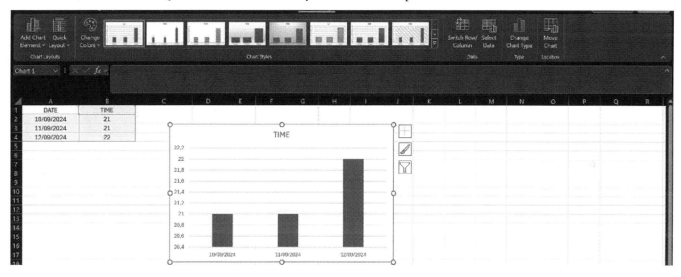

Adjusting the Style and Color

To make your chart reflect corporate branding or just to stand out more vividly, adjusting the color and style is essential. From the 'Chart Styles' options, you can choose from a variety of preset styles and color schemes that change your chart's look with a single click. For more specific branding, you can customize the chart colors by selecting the elements and choosing new fill colors, line colors, and effects from the 'Format' tab.

101

Enhancing Chart Readability with Data Labels and Markers

For line, scatter, or radar charts, adding markers can help to highlight individual data points. Similarly, data labels can display the data value near its point, making the charts easier to read and understand. This customization is especially helpful during presentations when viewers need to comprehend key figures at a glance.

Using Advanced Features Like Trendlines

For charts depicting data over time, adding a trendline can provide additional insight into the direction and speed of your data trends. Whether it's a linear, exponential, or moving average trendline, this feature can be effortlessly added from the 'Chart Elements' menu, providing a deeper analysis perspective.

Real-World Applications

Let's consider Michael, a marketing analyst, who uses these charting capabilities to prepare a monthly performance report for social media campaigns. By customizing his line charts to show both the trend of engagement rates and the precise data points using data labels, he provides clear, actionable insights to his team, helping them quickly assess the effectiveness of different strategies.

Consistency and Presentation

Finally, consistency in chart design ensures that when multiple charts are used in a proposal or report, they convey information without jarring the reader's visual flow. Consistency in elements like font styles, colors, and layout across all charts within a document speaks volumes about professionalism and attention to detail. From creation to customization, Excel offers not just tools but also a palette of possibilities to transform your data into compelling visual stories. It empowers you to not only present charts that are visually appealing but also construct them in ways that enhance your audience's understanding, making your data speak clearly and effectively, catered precisely to your narrative needs.

INTEGRATING TRENDLINES AND DATA LABELS

One of the most powerful ways to enhance the understanding and interpretability of data in Excel charts is through the use of trendlines and data labels. These features not only clarify what the data points represent but also highlight the overall direction or patterns that might not be immediately obvious.

Understanding and Applying Trendlines

Trendlines in Excel are statistical lines that smooth out data to show a pattern or trend more clearly. They can be a valuable tool in any chart that plots data in a scattered or line format. Whether you are looking at sales figures over several months or changes in traffic to a website, adding a trendline can help make sense of the fluctuations.

To add a trendline, simply click on the data series in your chart, and then navigate to 'Chart Elements' (the plus symbol next to the chart). Select 'Trendline' and choose the type of trendline that best fits your data. Excel offers several types, including linear, polynomial, and exponential. Each serves a different purpose: - **Linear trendlines** are best for simple, steadily increasing or decreasing data. - **Exponential trendlines** are suitable when data values rise or fall at increasingly higher rates. - **Polynomial trendlines** can model more complex data behaviors, with multiple rises and falls.

For example, a small business owner analyzing yearly sales data to predict future growth might use a polynomial trendline to account for unpredictable fluctuations in sales while still seeing the general upward or downward trend.

Enhancing Charts with Data Labels

Data labels offer a straightforward enhancement in your chart: they label data points with their actual data values or categories, making it easier for the viewer to identify what each point signifies without referring back to the axis scales. This is particularly useful in presentations or reports where the viewer needs to process information quickly.

Adding data labels is as simple as adding trendlines. Click on your chart, go to 'Chart Elements', and check 'Data Labels'. Excel provides options to position these labels in various places – center, top, bottom, left, or right of the data points, depending on what makes them most readable in the context of your specific chart.

Imagine a marketing manager tracking the performance of different advertising channels over several months. By using data labels, they can immediately see which months and which channels drove the most traffic, directly from the visual representation, without cross-referencing to separate data tables.

Customizing Trendlines and Data Labels

The power of these tools is not just in their ability to clarify but also in their flexibility. For trendlines, Excel allows you to format the line by changing its color, style, and thickness, making it stand out or blend in as needed. Moreover, you can extend the trendline forward or backward to project future data based on existing patterns. This feature is invaluable for forecasting and planning.

Data labels too can be formatted for better clarity and visual appeal. Font size, color, and box shape can be adjusted to make the labels clear and readable.

You can also choose to display additional information in the labels, such as the percentage change from the previous point, which can provide more depth to the analysis directly in the chart.

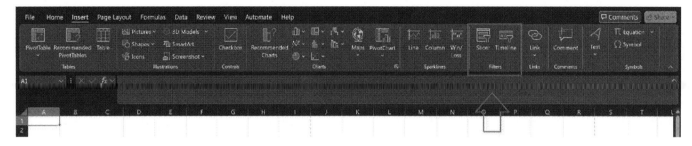

Practical Tips for Using Trendlines and Data Labels

1. **Keep It Relevant**: Only add trendlines and data labels if they add value to the interpretation of the chart. Overusing these features can clutter the visual space and make it harder to draw meaningful conclusions.

2. **Match the Trendline to the Data**: Choose the type of trendline that correctly reflects the pattern in your data. Misrepresentation can lead to incorrect interpretations.

3. **Use Data Labels Sparingly**: While data labels are helpful, too many can make your chart crowded. Use them primarily when the data points are not self-explanatory or when precise values are crucial for decision-making.

Real-World Applications

Consider a healthcare analyst reviewing patient recovery rates over several treatment cycles. By applying exponential trendlines, they can highlight the increasing effectiveness of a new treatment method. With data labels showing recovery rates at each cycle, the chart not only shows a trend but also offers exact figures at each point, making the data functional and immediately actionable.

By integrating trendlines and data labels, your Excel charts will not only carry more information but will also present this information in a way that is immediate and understandable, enhancing decision-making processes and communication. Whether in professional settings or personal projects, these tools transform raw data into clear visual stories, ready to support your objectives with precision and clarity.

EMPLOYING SPARKLINES FOR IMMEDIATE DATA VISUALIZATION

In the bustling world where quick decisions are the norm, Sparklines in Excel come as a significant relief, offering a micro-chart embedded directly within a worksheet cell. This feature provides a neat, concise way to show trends and variations associated with data in adjacent cells without occupying too much space. Sparklines make immediate data visualization possible, often illuminating patterns that are not immediately visible from raw data alone.

Introduction to Sparklines

Sparklines are tiny charts that fit in a single cell, each representing a series of data points chronologically. Introduced as a way to improve data analysis in Excel, they empower users to get a quick glimpse of the data trends at a glance.

There are three main types of Sparklines in Excel: Line, Column, and Win/Loss. Each type suits different data visualization needs: - **Line Sparklines** are useful for showing trends over time, such as monthly sales data. - **Column Sparklines** are best for comparing the magnitude of values, useful in inventory management to quickly see which items are most stocked. - **Win/Loss Sparklines** highlight positive, negative, or zero values, often used in financial statements to quickly spot gains and losses.

Creating Sparklines

To create a Sparkline, you first need the data that you want to visualize. Let's say you have monthly revenue data for the past year in a single row or column. Here's how you would create a Line Sparkline: 1. Select the cell where you want the Sparkline to appear. 2. Go to the 'Insert' tab and choose the type of Sparkline from the 'Sparklines' section. 3. In the dialog box that appears, select the range of cells that contain the data to visualize. 4. Click 'OK,' and a Sparkline appears, summarizing the data in the selected range in your chosen format.

Customizing Sparklines

After inserting Sparklines, customizing them can make them more informative and easier to understand. Excel allows you to adjust the color and style of the Sparkline, highlight particular points like high points, low points, or negative values, and change the axis settings. - To customize, select the cell containing the Sparkline and then adjust the settings from the 'Design' tab under 'Sparkline Tools' that appears. - You might change the color of the Sparkline to red if it represents financial data indicating a loss, or you may highlight the highest point to quickly draw attention to peak sales months.

Interpreting Sparklines

Interpreting Sparklines requires a basic understanding of the trends they represent. For instance, a downward trend in a Line Sparkline could indicate declining sales, needing quick managerial decisions. Similarly, sudden spikes in a Column Sparkline in inventory data might suggest stocking issues that require attention.

Practical Tips for Effective Sparklines

1. **Keep it Simple**: Since Sparklines are confined to a small space, simplicity is key. Too much customization can make them hard to read.
2. **Use Appropriate Scales**: When comparing Sparklines, ensure they all use the same scale for a fair comparison.
3. **Location Matters**: Position Sparklines near their corresponding data for context, making them easier to understand and analyze.

Real-World Application

Imagine a scenario in a retail store chain where regional managers need to quickly assess the performance of various stores. A report with Sparklines next to each store's sales data can instantly show which stores are performing well and which ones are not, assisting in efficient decision-making.

Laura, a supply chain analyst, uses Column Sparklines to monitor the stock levels of products across several warehouses. Each Sparkline provides an immediate visual summary of the inventory trends, helping her to manage reordering schedules effectively and avoid overstocking or stockouts.

Why Sparklines Matter

In today's fast-paced world, where data drives decisions, Sparklines offer a means to digest complex data swiftly. They transform traditional rows and columns of numbers into instantly comprehensible visuals, enabling quicker reactions and informed decisions. Whether in reports, dashboard summaries, or data-heavy documents, Sparklines serve as an essential tool for concise data visualization, proving that sometimes, the smallest enhancements in tools like Excel can bring about significant efficiencies in how we analyze and interpret data.

BOOK 3: EXCEL PROFICIENCY FOR ADVANCED USERS

CHAPTER 10: COMPLEX DATA MANAGEMENT TECHNIQUES

Welcome to a realm where Excel no longer just aids but transforms the way you manage data. In this chapter, we delve into complex data management techniques that push beyond the basics and guide you through mastering advanced functionalities that Excel 2024 offers.

Imagine you're at the helm of a ship navigating through the vast oceans of data in the corporate world, where each spreadsheet acts as a crucial navigational chart. The skills you're about to acquire are your advanced navigational tools—data validation to ensure the integrity of your data, techniques for seamless consolidation across multiple sheets, and methods to secure your worksheets and workbooks, safeguarding your valuable information like the precious cargo it is.

By this stage of our journey together, you are no longer just participating in data entry or simple manipulations. You are moving towards a strategic role, using Excel to enforce data policies, streamline operations, and protect information. You'll learn how to employ data validation rules that act as quality checks, automatically barring incorrect entries that could lead to costly mistakes. Imagine setting up a system that ensures every entry into your financial reports is within expected ranges, preventing any abnormalities long before they become visible in charts or summaries.

Consolidation techniques will become your best ally when dealing with reports from various departments. You'll easily merge data from different teams into a cohesive whole, providing a comprehensive overview necessary for strategic decision-making. Think of it as gathering all pieces of a puzzle rapidly and efficiently, seeing the big picture without laboriously examining every tiny fragment.

Lastly, securing your Excel files will no longer be a mere afterthought but a robust strategy. As you reinforce the protection of your spreadsheets, consider yourself a gatekeeper, holding the key to critical data that, if exposed or altered, could undermine your projects or business operations.

By the end of this chapter, equipped with these sophisticated tools and techniques, you will be prepared to tackle complex data challenges head-on, ensuring accuracy, consistency, and security in your data management practices. This knowledge doesn't just make you proficient in Excel; it makes you an indispensable part of your team or organization, armed with the skills to turn data into a powerful advantage.

ENFORCING DATA INTEGRITY THROUGH VALIDATION RULES

Data integrity is the keystone in any system where data is critical to decisions, strategy, and outcomes. In high-stakes environments, one erroneous entry can propagate through your projects with far-reaching consequences. Mastering Excel's data validation rules is akin to setting up a highly trained guard at the gates of your data fortress—a meticulous filter that ensures only the correct data enters your domains.

Understanding Data Validation

Data validation in Excel is a powerful feature that does more than just restrict what can be entered into the cells of your worksheets. It is your first line of defense, ensuring that the input received is accurate, thereby maintaining the quality of your data with minimal effort.

At its core, data validation is about defining the criteria that your data must meet. Whether it's ensuring a date falls within a specific range, a number exceeds a minimum value, or text contains a certain number of characters, Excel's data validation tools enable you to establish these rules effortlessly.

Setting Up Basic Validation Rules

Starting with simple criteria, imagine you have a spreadsheet managing event registrations, and you need to ensure that no participant can register before a certain date or after a deadline. Here's how you would set this up:

1. **Select the cells** where the dates will be entered.
2. Go to **Data** on the Ribbon.
3. Click **Data Validation**.
4. In the Data Validation dialog box, under the **Settings** tab, select **Date** in the Allow list.
5. In the Data box, choose the condition (e.g., 'between').
6. Enter the **start** and **end dates** for your criteria.

Now, any date entered outside this range will trigger an alert, and the user will be unable to proceed until a valid date is provided.

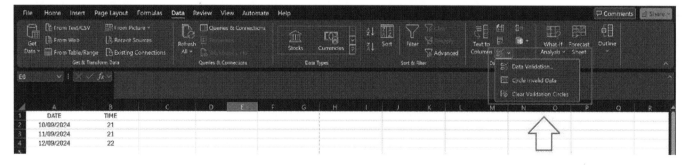

Expanding to More Complex Criteria

As your needs become more intricate, Excel's data validation rules can be enhanced using formulas. Suppose you are managing a budget and need to ensure that departmental expenses do not exceed their allocated budget within a spreadsheet. You can set up a validation rule that compares entered expenses against a budget cap set in another cell.

1. Select the cells where expense amounts are entered.
2. Open the Data Validation dialog box.
3. Set the Allow field to **Custom**.

4. Enter a formula that references the budget cap cell, such as =A1<B1, where A1 is the cell containing the expense entry and B1 is the budget cap.

This setup ensures real-time compliance with budget restrictions, enforcing financial discipline directly within your data entry processes.

Handling Errors with Grace

When data integrity is at stake, communicating errors effectively is as crucial as preventing them. Excel allows you to customize the messages that appear when someone tries to enter invalid data. Configuring a helpful error message involves:

1. Staying in the **Data Validation** dialog box.
2. Switch to the **Error Alert** tab.
3. Choose the style of the alert (Stop, Warning, or Information).
4. Write a clear, concise title and error message that explains how to correct the mistake.

Consider an inventory sheet where specific items must be entered in defined quantities. A clear message like, "Please enter a quantity multiple of 10" guides the user more effectively than a generic error prompt.

Real-World Applications: Securing High-Quality Data Entry

Let's illustrate with a real-world scenario: A pharmaceutical company uses an Excel sheet to track medication stocks. Each drug has a minimum and maximum stock requirement. By implementing data validation rules, the system ensures that each entry adheres to these thresholds, thereby preventing potential overstock or stockout situations.

The data validation rule would be set to ensure the stock number is within the specified range for each medication. This direct enforcement of stock policies mitigates risks associated with manual monitoring and human error.

Tips for Advanced Data Validation

- **Dropdown Lists**: For fields that require standard responses, such as department names or locations, setting up dropdown lists ensures uniformity in data entry.

- **Regular Expressions**: For more advanced users, integrating regular expressions through VBA can validate complex patterns like email addresses or phone numbers.

- **Combine with Conditional Formatting**: To make data validation visually intuitive, couple it with conditional formatting to highlight cells that need attention.

By setting structured but flexible barriers to entry, Excel's data validation tools help maintain the integrity and reliability of your data ecosystem. These rules not only safeguard your data but also streamline the process of identifying and correcting errors, thereby enhancing overall efficiency and reliability in your operations. Through diligent application of these methods, you can harness the full potential of Excel to manage data effectively, ensuring your work stands up to scrutiny under any criteria.

DATA CONSOLIDATION ACROSS MULTIPLE SHEETS

In a world swamped with data, having a solid grip on how to streamline this vast information across numerous Excel worksheets is a defining skill. Data consolidation is not just about merging sheets; it's a symphony of aligning, summarizing, and interlinking varied data into a unified format that's comprehensive and analyzable. This section is designed to equip you with advanced techniques to consolidate data across multiple sheets effectively, making this complex process a straightforward and error-free one.

Why Consolidate Data?

Start by imagining you're at the crossroads of multiple information streams. Each Excel sheet from different departments represents a tributary of data flowing into a larger data lake. Your task? Create a cohesive overview that enables strategic decision-making without the need to manually navigate through each sheet every time a question arises. Whether it's monthly sales, regional revenues, or customer feedback across various platforms, consolidating this data not only saves time but significantly enhances your analytical capabilities.

The Essentials of Data Consolidation

Data consolidation in Excel allows you to pull together diverse data sets into a single location where combined reports and analyses can be generated. Excel facilitates this through several features and techniques which, when mastered, can handle vast amounts of data with reliability and ease.

Direct Link Consolidation

When you want to keep your data connected to its source, so any updates in the primary sheets automatically reflect in your master sheet, direct link consolidation is your go-to method. Here's how this plays out practically:

1. **Create a Master Sheet**: This will be your consolidation hub.
2. **Use Formulas to Reference Other Sheets**: For example, if you want to sum sales from different sheets named East, West, and Central, you use a formula in your master sheet such as =SUM(East!B2, West!B2, Central!B2).

This method ensures that your master sheet always reflects the current scenario across all connected sheets, perfect for dynamic environments where data updates frequently.

Consolidation by Position

When the data setups in all the sheets are identical, i.e., the layouts mirror each other, consolidation by position is highly efficient. This becomes valuable in scenarios like consolidating annual financial statements where each sheet from every department follows the same template.

In Excel, you may perform this action using the Consolidate tool: - **Select the target area in your master sheet** where you want the summarization. - Navigate to **Data > Consolidate**. - Choose your function (e.g., Sum, Average) and add references from each sheet to be considered. - Click OK and watch as Excel merges the data based on their positions in their respective sheets.

Using Pivot Tables for Consolidation

For those who need powerful, flexible consolidation with the ability to easily tweak which data pieces are being summarized and how they are displayed, Pivot Tables are the answer. Here's a quick way to use Pivot Tables for consolidating data:

- Gather all data ranges you want to include in your Pivot Table.
- Create a new Worksheet and insert a Pivot Table.
- Select your data ranges from different sheets, and set them up in the Pivot Table fields pane, adjusting filters, columns, rows, and values as needed.

Pivot Tables are particularly useful for interactive, complex data consolidation tasks where you might need to drill down into specifics or reconfigure the data display dynamically.

Practical Tips for Effective Data Consolidation

- **Ensure Uniformity**: Before consolidation, make sure that all data formats across sheets are uniform to avoid any errors or misinterpretations.

- **Verify Data Ranges**: Always double-check the ranges selected for consolidation to ensure no data is missed or incorrectly included.
- **Create Data Backups**: Before performing consolidation, especially if using direct methods that alter the layout or data, ensure you have backups to prevent loss of information.

Real-World Application: Consolidating Sales Data

Consider the task faced by a sales manager who needs to compile quarterly sales data spread out across multiple regional sheets. By utilizing the Consolidate tool in Excel, the manager quickly aggregates the total sales from each region, analyzes trends, and prepares a comprehensive report for the leadership—turning disparate data into actionable intelligence.

Utilizing these sophisticated data consolidation techniques allows you to harness Excel's full potential to streamline workflows, improve data accuracy, and provide more impactful data analysis. It morphs the challenge of handling multiple data streams into a strategic advantage, empowering you to make more informed decisions swiftly and effectively.

STREAMLINING DATA IMPORT FROM EXTERNAL SOURCES

In the world of data management, the ability to seamlessly import data from various external sources into Excel is a capability akin to translating multiple languages fluently. For advanced Excel users, mastering this skill means significant efficiency in handling diverse datasets, ensuring data-driven decisions are backed by comprehensive, accurate, and up-to-date information.

Understanding Data Import Dynamics

The process of importing data might seem straightforward initially, but complexities arise due to the varied formats and sources data can stream in from—be it databases, online services, or other software applications. Each source speaks a 'different dialect' of data, and Excel has built-in tools to translate these dialects into a language it understands. This integration can streamline workflows, enhance productivity, and eliminate the manual drudgery that often comes with data handling.

Step-by-Step Guide to Importing Data

The process differs slightly depending on the source, but the fundamental steps largely remain consistent. Let's explore these using a common scenario: Importing data from a SQL database and a CSV file, as these are prevalent sources of external data.

Importing from a SQL Database

1. **Initiate the Data Import Wizard**: Access this via the Data tab in Excel; select 'From Other Sources' and then 'From SQL Server'.

2. **Connect to the Database**: Provide the necessary connection details, including server name and database credentials.

3. **Select the Data**: Specify the tables or use SQL queries to determine which data to import.

4. **Finalize the Import**: Configure any final options like refreshing data on open or at specific time intervals and finish the setup.

Once your data is imported, it appears in a table format, and Excel allows you to treat it like any other data—filtering, sorting, and computing as needed.

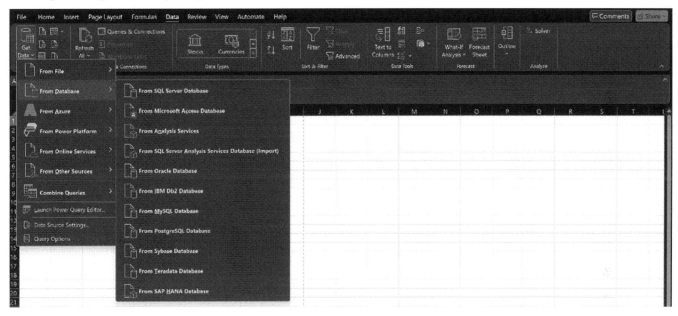

Importing from CSV Files

1. **Open the Import Dialog**: Choose the 'From Text/CSV' option under the Data tab.

2. **Find Your File**: Navigate to where your CSV file is stored and select it.

3. **Set Import Preferences**: Excel will often provide a preview of the data. Here, you can specify delimiters and data types to ensure the data is parsed correctly.

4. **Complete the Import**: Once configured, import the data which will then be available as a regular Excel sheet.

These steps handle most basic scenarios you might encounter when importing data into Excel.

Streamlining Complex Imports

When dealing with more complex or frequent data imports, Excel's Power Query is an indispensable tool. It offers advanced query capabilities, and transformation options overlooked in the basic import utility—ideal for scenarios requiring repetitive, complex data manipulation.

Utilizing Power Query for Enhanced Data Import

- **Access Power Query**: Navigate to the Data tab and select 'Get Data'.
- **Choose the Data Source**: Power Query supports numerous sources, from web pages to databases, and even folder directories.
- **Transform Data**: Before finalizing the import, Power Query lets you manipulate the data—be it removing columns, changing data types, or merging tables.
- **Load Data**: Once your data is refined and ready, load it directly into your Excel workbook.

Power Query not only simplifies the process but also automates data updates. You set up queries once and refresh them with just a click whenever you need updated data.

Practical Tips for Efficient Data Imports

- **Regularly Update Connections**: Data sources evolve, and so should your connections. Regular checks ensure your data links are not broken and data remains accurate.
- **Use Connection Properties**: Tailor your data updates (refresh rate, query definition, etc.) to suit your needs, ensuring you're always working with the most relevant data.
- **Organize Imported Data**: Especially when handling large volumes, use Excel's Table designs or PivotTables to better organize and summarize imported data.

Real-World Application: Enhancing Business Decisions

Consider a retail company analyzing customer feedback from multiple channels. By importing data regularly into Excel from these disparate sources, the company can quickly aggregate feedback, identify trends, and react promptly to customer needs—turning raw data into actionable insights.

By mastering data import techniques in Excel, you transform raw, external data into strategic assets. This capability is critical not just for maintaining operational effectiveness but also for reinforcing the reliability and decision-making prowess within your organization. In the vast seas of data we navigate today, being able to efficiently import and manage this data in Excel is not just a skill but a strategic imperative.

SECURING WORKSHEETS AND WORKBOOKS

In the landscape of modern data management, securing your Excel worksheets and workbooks is paramount. It's not merely about keeping the data away from unauthorized access; it's about ensuring the integrity and confidentiality of the information your business operates upon daily. As you delve deeper into Excel's capabilities, understanding these security measures becomes crucial, especially when handling sensitive or proprietary data.

Understanding the Need for Security

Consider your Excel files as vaults containing valuable assets of your business intelligence. Just as a vault's security is critical to safeguarding its contents, so too is the protection of your Excel data against potential threats such as unintentional data alteration or unauthorized access. This subchapter will guide you through the practical steps to secure your Excel worksheets and workbooks effectively, providing you with both peace of mind and compliance with data protection standards.

Protecting Your Worksheets

Securing a worksheet in Excel means locking it down so that unintended changes cannot be made—whether it's from an external party or from a colleague who might not be aware of the data's complexity. Here's how you can fortify your worksheet efficiently:

1. **Open the Worksheet Protection Dialog**: Navigate to the 'Review' tab in Excel and click on 'Protect Sheet.'

2. **Set Your Parameters**: You'll be presented with several options like allowing users to select locked cells, format cells, sort data, etc. Choose according to your need.

3. **Enter a Password**: This is optional but recommended for higher security. Once set, the password will be required to unprotect the sheet.

Remember, protecting a worksheet primarily controls how the cells can be manipulated but doesn't prevent the viewing of its content.

Workbook Protection

While worksheet protection focuses on individual sheets within a workbook, protecting the entire workbook encapsulates broader safeguards. It ensures the structure of the workbook remains intact—no adding, moving, or deleting sheets.

To protect your workbook: - Navigate to the 'Review' tab and select 'Protect Workbook.' - Choose 'Protect Workbook for Structure and Windows.' The 'Structure' option prevents altering the workbook's architecture, while 'Windows' maintains the size and position of the workbook's window. - Set a password if desired to enforce this protection.

Advanced Security with File Encryption

For confidentiality that surpasses simple protection, file encryption is your go-to. Excel offers an advanced feature where you can encrypt the file, requiring a password to open the document itself.

To encrypt your workbook: - Go to 'File' and choose 'Info.' - Click on 'Protect Workbook,' then select 'Encrypt with Password.' - Enter a strong password. Once set, this password will be necessary to access the workbook at all.

Encrypting your file provides a robust layer of security, ensuring that even if the file lands into the wrong hands, the data remains unreadable without the correct password.

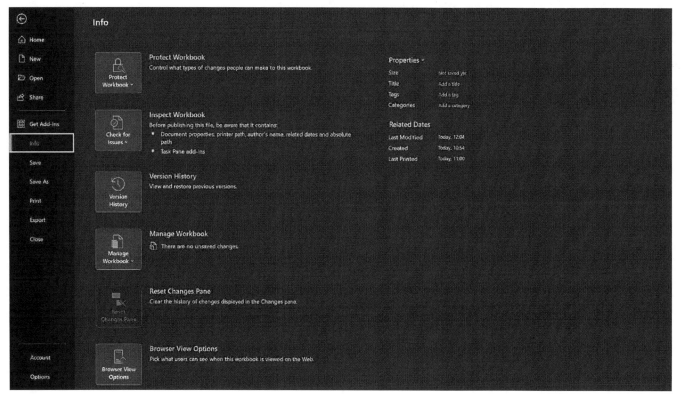

Backing Up Securely

While not a direct form of protection, ensuring that you have secure backups of your data can save immense time and prevent data loss. Regularly back up your secured Excel files to an external drive or secure cloud service. This way, even in the case of physical damage to your machine or data corruption, you can restore your valuable work with minimal disruption.

Real-World Application: Financial Data Security

Imagine you are managing the financial records of a small business where multiple individuals access the Excel workbook containing sensitive fiscal information. By implementing worksheet protection, you ensure that formulas and cell formats remain untouched, preventing costly errors. Encrypting the file secures the contents from prying eyes, making sure that only authorized personnel can view or modify the financial data.

Practical Tips for Effective Data Security

- **Regularly Update Passwords**: Changing passwords periodically helps in maintaining the security integrity of your data.
- **Educate Your Team**: Ensure that everyone understands the importance of data security and knows how to handle protected documents correctly.
- **Audit Access and Modifications**: Keep track of who accesses the data and what changes are made, especially in a collaborative environment.

Securing your Excel data effectively buffers your operations from potential threats and errors, ensuring the integrity and privacy of your critical business insights. By adopting these measures, you equip yourself with not just the tools for data protection but also the confidence that your data management practices are robust and secure.

Chapter 11: Complex Formulas and Functional Expertise

As we venture deeper into the realms of Excel, we embrace the challenge of complex formulas and functional expertise in Chapter 11. You've already climbed the formidable slopes of conditional formatting, basic formulas, and intermediate data analysis techniques. Now, it's time to scale the heights that will truly distinguish you as an Excel expert.

Navigating through Excel's advanced functionalities, think of yourself not just as a user, but as a craftsman. Each formula, every function you learn is a tool in your arsenal, shaping raw data into insightful, actionable information. As we embark on this journey, we delve into array formulas, a powerhouse for handling voluminous data operations with a finescale preciseness that simple formulas cannot achieve.

Consider the scenario of managing sales data across multiple product lines and geographies. With array formulas, what once took several steps and multiple recalculations simplifies into a single, elegant solution. This not only saves time but reduces the margin for error, allowing for more dynamic data interaction.

Transitioning from arrays, we explore the nuanced art of nested functions. Imagine layering functions like a skilled chef combining ingredients, where each layer adds depth and flavor, transforming simple numbers into rich, textured decisions. These are not just computational steps but strategic tools that enhance your problem-solving capabilities.

Through real-world examples, such as budget forecasting and complex inventory tracking, we will see how nested functions and sophisticated formulas like SUMIFS, COUNTIFS, INDEX, and MATCH turn complex challenges into clear, manageable tasks. These examples aren't just exercises; they're common scenarios you'll encounter in the world of business analytics and data management.

As you engage with this chapter, remember that mastering these advanced tools will not only boost your productivity but also elevate your professional value, making you a pivotal asset in any data-driven decision-making process. Let's embrace these advanced features with confidence, propelling your Excel skills towards true technical artistry.

Working with Array Formulas

Array formulas in Excel are like a Swiss Army knife for data analysts – multifunctional and indispensable in scenarios dealing with large datasets that require simultaneous calculations across multiple cells. As we explore their unique capabilities, we'll transform your Excel proficiency, turning complex data tasks into straightforward operations.

Why Array Formulas?

Imagine you're faced with a spreadsheet filled with sales data across various products and regions. You need to calculate the total sales for each product across different regions without creating multiple temporary columns or manual summing. This is where array formulas come into play, performing bulk operations on data arrays with a single, powerful formula.

Understanding Array Formulas

In essence, an array formula can perform multiple calculations on one or more items in an array. They can return either a single result or multiple results. Traditional formulas process only a single value at any given time, whereas array formulas handle entire arrays of data at once.

Creating Your First Array Formula

Let's dive into a practical scenario. Suppose you have a table listing quantities and respective unit prices of products. To find the total value for each product, you would traditionally multiply quantities and unit prices line by line.

Using an array formula, you can simplify this process: 1. First, select the range where you want the total prices to appear. 2. Enter =array1   array2, replacing array1 and array2 with the actual ranges for quantity and unit price. 3. Instead of pressing Enter as usual, you'll finalize the array formula by pressing Ctrl+Shift+Enter. Excel recognizes it as an array formula and encloses it in curly braces {}.

Handling More Complex Scenarios

Array formulas aren't limited to simple arithmetic. They shine in more complicated scenarios where you need to prune data based on multiple conditions. For instance, if you want to count how many sales transactions were over $500 but only if they occurred in certain regions, array formulas make it feasible without flustering through numerous steps.

Array Formula Limitations and Solutions

One common struggle with array formulas is managing errors. Due to their complex nature, if one part of an array formula fails, typically the whole formula returns an error. To troubleshoot, check each component of the formula independently by isolating segments of the array formula in separate cells to ensure they work correctly.

Moreover, heavy use of array formulas can slow down your workbook due to the computation needed. To maintain performance, use them judiciously and consider alternative methods like PivotTables or built-in functions if applicable.

Integrating Array Formulas in Reports

Beyond calculations, array formulas can be transformative in automated reports. For instance, you can use an array formula to conditionally sum data by month, product, or other criteria, seamlessly integrating dynamic summaries into your report without manual intervention every time the data updates.

Advanced Tips with Array Formulas

- **Use Named Ranges**: To make your array formulas simpler and easier to understand, use named ranges within your array formulas. This approach not only clarifies what the formula is referencing but also makes it easier to manage your data as it grows.
- **Combine with Other Functions**: Don't hesitate to merge array formulas with other powerful Excel functions. For example, combining IF statements within your array formulas can filter which data gets processed, adding a layer of decision-making to your data handling process.
- **Testing and Error Checking**: Always test array formulas in a controlled environment before applying them to critical operational data. This practice helps you understand the output and refine the formula as needed without risking data integrity.

Embracing the Power of Arrays

Embracing array formulas is akin to upgrading your data toolset – it's about making strides from manual, time-consuming data handling to automated, efficient data management. As you refine your skills with these functions, you not only save time but also unlock new possibilities for data analysis and reporting.

By understanding and applying array formulas, you're setting yourself apart in the world of data manipulation. Remember, the goal here isn't just to learn but to apply these skills to make your data work for you, creating more insightful, impactful reports and analyses that were once thought too complex to tackle manually.

IMPLEMENTING NESTED FUNCTIONS FOR INTRICATE CALCULATIONS

The mastery of nested functions is akin to learning a form of high-level Excel sorcery. It's about merging multiple tools into one potent solution, handling a variety of challenging scenarios with grace and precision. In this section, we delve into the strategic application of nested functions for intricate calculations, transforming data analysis complexities into simple, manageable tasks.

The Art of Nesting in Excel

Nesting involves placing one or more Excel functions inside another, like Russian dolls. This structure creates robust solutions where the output of one function becomes the input for another, extending Excel's capability beyond its basic function limits.

To illustrate, imagine you're faced with a conditional scenario where multiple criteria need to validate to trigger a specific calculation or result. A nested function allows you to weigh numerous conditions within a single formula, streamlining processes and enhancing your worksheet's computational power.

Constructing a Basic Nested Formula

Let's set the groundwork with a simple example – calculating a conditional sum that depends on multiple criteria. Suppose you need to calculate bonuses for employees based on their sales figures; the bonus depends on the bracket within which their sales total falls.

A traditional approach might involve multiple steps or separate calculations, but with nested functions, you can consolidate this into a single, efficient formula combining IF and SUM. Here's a simplified view:

1. **Identify the conditions:** Define what each sales bracket is and the corresponding bonus.
2. **Set up the IF function:** This function checks whether the condition (sales bracket) is met.
3. **Embed the SUM function:** Inside the condition, sum the total sales to calculate the bonus.

Here's how the formula might look:

excel =IF(SUM(sales_range) > 10000, Bonus_Level_1, IF(SUM(sales_range) > 5000, Bonus_Level_2, Bonus_Level_3))

Growing Complexity with Real-world Applications

As your confidence grows, so too will the complexity of the tasks you manage with nested functions. Consider a more complex example: You need to determine the inventory reordering levels based on multiple factors, including seasonality, existing inventory levels, and predicted sales growth.

This scenario might require nesting multiple IF, AND, and OR functions together, providing a highly customized logic tree that dynamically adjusts reorder levels by product category and season.

Advanced Nesting: Combining Logical and Lookup Functions

Moving deeper, Excel allows you to mix different types of functions within your nests. For instance, you can combine logical functions (IF, AND, OR) with lookup functions (VLOOKUP, INDEX, MATCH) to perform sophisticated data intersections and extractions.

Imagine a scenario where you need to fetch the price of a product only if it meets specific criteria regarding availability and vendor rating. Here's a structure you might use:

excel =IF(AND(VLOOKUP(product_code, Products!$A$1:$F$100, 3, FALSE) > 20, VLOOKUP(product_code, Products!$A$1:$F$100, 5, FALSE) >= 4), VLOOKUP(product_code, Products!$A$1:$F$100, 6, FALSE), "Check Availability")

This formula first checks product availability and vendor rating. If both conditions are satisfied, it fetches the price; otherwise, it signals to check availability.

Best Practices for Using Nested Functions

- **Keep it readable:** While Excel allows you to nest up to 64 levels deep, keeping your formulas readable is paramount. Aim for clarity, not just complexity.

- **Calculate separately:** When building complex formulas, test each nested function separately to ensure accuracy before combining them.

- **Document your formulas:** Use comments and structured naming within your workbook to clarify the purpose of each formula, especially when using nested structures.

Troubleshooting Common Issues

Errors in nested formulas can be daunting to decode due to their complexity. Here's how to approach troubleshooting:

- **Break down the formula:** Split the nested formula into parts and test each segment separately in adjacent cells.

- **Use error-checking tools:** Excel's formula auditing tools can help trace errors and show dependencies clearly, aiding in pinpointing mistakes.

Leveraging Nested Functions for Data Insights

The true power of nested functions lies in their ability to produce actionable insights from complex data sets with minimal manual intervention. By mastering this advanced skill, you escalate your role from a data processor to a strategic analyst, capable of influencing business decisions through insightful data manipulation. As you continue to practice and apply these principles, remember that nested functions are not just about handling data more efficiently—they're about viewing data challenges through a lens of creative problem solving, where each layer of the function adds depth and precision to your analysis.

CONDITIONAL SUMMING AND COUNTING WITH SUMIFS AND COUNTIFS

In the advanced arena of Excel, SUMIFS and COUNTIFS stand as the vigilant guardians of data integrity, ensuring that you can extract precisely filtered sums and counts based on specific, multiple criteria, all from massive datasets. Let's explore how these functions can transform your approach to data analysis and why they're indispensable for advanced Excel users.

The Essence of SUMIFS and COUNTIFS

Imagine you're overseeing a regional sales report which requires you to not only report total sales but also dissect these figures based by product type, time periods, or geographical regions.

Using SUMIFS and COUNTIFS, you can pull these figures swiftly without manual sorting or excessive intermediate steps, directly improving productivity and data reliability.

Harnessing SUMIFS for Conditional Summing

Let's begin with SUMIFS. This function is designed to sum values in a range depending on multiple criteria. For instance, if you wanted to calculate the total sales of a specific product in a specific region during a specific timeframe, SUMIFS makes this task manageable.

To put this into practice, consider this scenario: You are tasked with finding the total sales of 'Product A' in 'Region North' during 'Q1'. You have a table where each row represents a sale, showing product, region, date, and sale amount.

excel =SUMIFS(Sale_Amounts, Products, "Product A", Regions, "Region North", Sales_Dates, ">="&DATE(2022,1,1), Sales_Dates, "<="&DATE(2022,3,31))

This formula demonstrates the power of SUMIFS: - Sale_Amounts is the range of cells that contains the data to sum. - Each pair of criteria range and criteria (Products, "Product A", Regions, "Region North", etc.) pinpoints the specific subset of data to include in the sum.

Mastering COUNTIFS for Conditional Counting

Now, switching gears to COUNTIFS—this function is similar to SUMIFS but counts the number of times certain criteria are met instead of summing values. This is particularly useful when you need to understand volume rather than value.

For example, how many sales transactions occurred for 'Product A' in 'Region North' during 'Q1'? The setup of COUNTIFS is analogous to SUMIFS:

excel =COUNTIFS(Products, "Product A", Regions, "Region North", Sales_Dates, ">="&DATE(2022,1,1), Sales_Dates, "<="&DATE(2022,3,31))

In this instance: - Each criteria range and criteria define which rows are counted based on matching those specified conditions.

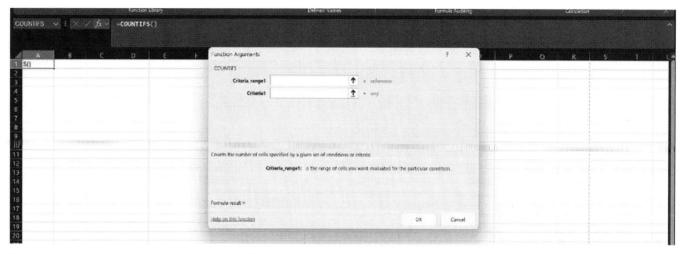

Practical Considerations: Tips for Effective Use

1. **Ensure Accuracy in Criteria**: Mistakes in specifying criteria are common pitfalls. Verify that the criteria exactly match the data entries. For dates and numerical ranges, ensure your logical operators (>=, <=) are correctly placed.

2. **Optimize for Large Datasets**: While powerful, these functions can slow down Excel when used on exceptionally large datasets. To mitigate performance hits, try to limit the range to the necessary rows rather than entire columns.

3. **Document Your Formulas**: As your formulas grow complex, keep track of what each part does. Adding comments within your Excel workbook can aid you or anyone else who needs to understand or modify your work later.

Troubleshooting Common Errors

- **Mismatched Range Sizes**: Your criteria ranges must match the sum range or count range in size. Inconsistencies here will result in errors.

- **Incorrect Data Types**: Ensure that the data format in your criteria matches the data format in the range. For example, dates should be compared with dates.

Leveraging SUMIFS and COUNTIFS for Insightful Reporting

Advanced applications of SUMIFS and COUNTIFS can feed directly into dynamic reports and dashboards, providing real-time insights into performance metrics, operational efficiencies, or market trends. As you get comfortable with these functions, you will start to see opportunities everywhere to drive data-driven decision-making processes.

In essence, SUMIFS and COUNTIFS are not merely functions; they are gateways to deeper data analysis, allowing you to navigate through enormous datasets with incredible specificity and accuracy. Their ability to filter and compute on the fly makes them invaluable tools in your Excel toolkit, ensuring you're prepared for any analytical challenge that comes your way.

DYNAMIC DATA LOOKUP WITH INDEX AND MATCH

In the journey through Excel's powerful capabilities, mastering the art of dynamic data lookup using INDEX and MATCH functions is akin to unlocking a new level of data manipulation sophistication. These functions, individually mighty and when paired, potent, allow you to retrieve information from a dataset based on complex, dynamic criteria, providing flexibility and precision that the widely used VLOOKUP can seldom match.

Understanding the Power of INDEX and MATCH

The INDEX function returns the value of an element in a table or array, given its row and column number. MATCH, on the other hand, is used to find the relative position of an item in an array that matches a specified value. When combined, these functions can look up values in a two-dimensional table, maneuvering through rows and columns with agility—providing a solution that adapts dynamically to your data's structure.

Why Prefer INDEX and MATCH Over VLOOKUP?

While VLOOKUP is straightforward and popular, it comes with limitations—most notably, its inability to look to the left (it only searches rightward from the key value) and its dependency on static column references in formulas. This can lead to errors and inefficiencies, especially in dynamic datasets where columns might be added or removed.

INDEX and MATCH conquer these shortcomings gracefully, allowing:

- **Bidirectional Lookups**: They can retrieve data to the left or right of the lookup value.
- **Dynamic Column Referencing**: As your data changes, your formulas adjust without manual recalibration.

Setting Up INDEX and MATCH

Imagine you have a sales record with columns for Date, Product ID, and Sales Volume. If you need to find the sales volume for a specific product on a given date, where columns may be added or rearranged, INDEX and MATCH offer the flexibility needed.

To retrieve the Sales Volume for a specific Product ID, the formula structure would look something like this:

excel =INDEX(Sales_Volume_Column, MATCH(Target_Product_ID, Product_ID_Column, 0))

Here's a breakdown: - **INDEX(Sales *Volume* Column...)**: This part of the formula specifies where the return value will come from. Sales_Volume_Column is the range containing the sales data. - **MATCH(Target *Product* ID, Product *ID* Column, 0)**: This function searches for Target_Product_ID within the Product_ID_Column. The 0 denotes an exact match, essential for precise lookups.

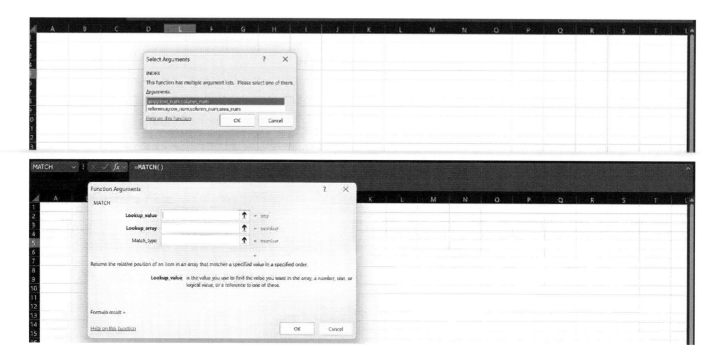

Practical Tips for Implementing INDEX and MATCH

- **Exact Ranges**: Ensure that the ranges specified in MATCH are accurate and match the corresponding range in INDEX in size and shape. Any mismatch can lead to incorrect results or errors.

- **Handling Errors**: Wrap your formula in IFERROR to handle cases where MATCH does not find a value, which prevents your Excel sheet from displaying unprofessional error codes.

- **Dynamic Range Referencing**: Utilize named ranges or table references to make your formulas more readable and resistant to errors caused by data structure changes.

Troubleshooting Common Challenges

Sometimes, even well-set formulas might not return the expected results. Consider these troubleshooting steps: - **Verify Match Type**: Always ensure the third argument in MATCH is appropriate—0 for exact match is typical, but 1 and -1 can be used for approximate matches under specific sorted data conditions. - **Check for Duplicates**: MATCH will return the position of the first occurrence if duplicates exist. Ensure your lookup values are unique or adjust your strategy to account for multiples. - **Data Format Consistency**: Mismatched data formats (e.g., text formatted as numbers) can lead to failed matches. Ensure consistency in your columns.

Advanced Applications

Once comfortable with the basics, experiment with more complex arrangements. For instance, reversing the order of MATCH to perform a reverse lookup (rightmost to leftmost) or nesting multiple MATCH functions to handle multi-criteria lookups.

Beyond Just Retrieving Data

INDEX and MATCH don't just retrieve values; they allow for dynamic interactions with your data. As you progress in your Excel mastery, using these functions strategically can lead to impressive efficiencies and deeper data insights, aiding in decision-making processes where adaptability and precision are crucial.

In conclusion, the combined strength of INDEX and MATCH functions offers a robust framework for dealing with intricate, variable data sets, where traditional lookup functions falter. Understanding and applying these tools proficiently means enhancing not only the flexibility of your spreadsheets but also the effectiveness of your data analysis capabilities. As you continue to build on your Excel skills, remember that each function learned not only adds a tool to your repertoire but also layers of depth to your analytical abilities.

CHAPTER 12: EXCEL MACRO UTILIZATION

Welcome to a transformative journey into the world of Excel macros—an area where Excel not only supports your data management tasks but also automates them, freeing up your valuable time for more strategic activities. As you step into this advanced realm with Chapter 12, be prepared to unlock the powerful capabilities that Excel macros offer.

Think of Excel macros as your personal assistants in the world of data management. They handle repetitive tasks with precision and without fatigue, executing complex sequences with a simple trigger. Whether it's repetitive data entry, formatting tasks, or complex calculation sequences, macros can do these efficiently, leaving zero room for the human errors that sometimes sneak in during manual processes.

Let us start with a real-world scenario to illustrate the power of macros. Imagine you're tasked with generating monthly reports from several datasets. Normally, this involves extracting data, performing calculations, formatting the results, and then presenting these in a report—a time-consuming process, right? Now imagine scripting a macro that automates all these steps. With a single click, your report is prepared, formatted, and ready for presentation. This not only saves time but also ensures consistency across reports.

As you progress through this chapter, you'll learn not only how to record these helpful macros but also how to tweak and refine them for optimal performance. We'll guide you through writing your first script in Visual Basic for Applications (VBA), the backbone behind Excel macros. This might sound daunting, but remember, every Excel master was once a beginner. With clear, step-by-step instructions and practical tips, you'll gain the confidence to craft custom macros tailored to your specific needs.

Furthermore, as you become more comfortable with basic macros, we'll explore how to create macro-driven interface elements, enhancing the interactivity and user-friendliness of your Excel workbooks. By the end of this chapter, not only will your productivity have skyrocketed, but you'll also view Excel as a more powerful tool that does far more than mere data entry and analysis.

Harnessing the power of Excel macros is like turning a key to unlock a new level of data management efficiency. Let's turn that key together and watch as new horizons in Excel proficiency unfold before us.

MACRO BASICS: RECORDING AND UTILIZATION

Embarking on the path to mastering Excel macros begins with understanding the basics of recording and utilizing these powerful automation tools. Macros can significantly enhance your productivity by performing routine tasks with the press of a button—like a faithful assistant who works tirelessly behind the scenes.

Recording Your First Macro

Your journey starts in the Developer tab in Excel, a place where magic begins. If this tab isn't already visible, you can easily activate it by going to File -> Options -> Customize Ribbon and then checking the box next to Developer in the right column. This tab is your gateway to creating and managing macros.

Now, let's record our first macro. Imagine you perform a set of actions frequently, such as formatting sales data every week. By recording a macro as you perform these actions once, Excel can replicate them whenever needed.

1. Prepare your data in Excel as you normally would before applying any repetitive formatting or calculations.

2. Navigate to the Developer tab, click 'Record Macro', and a small dialog box pops up asking you to name your macro. Choose a clear, descriptive name without spaces—for instance, "FormatSalesData".

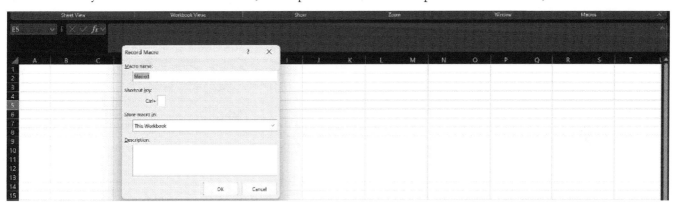

3. It's also prudent to assign a shortcut key at this point, but ensure it doesn't override any default Excel shortcuts. An example could be Ctrl+Shift+F.

4. Select where to store your macro. The simplest option is "This Workbook," but if you intend to use this macro across multiple workbooks, choose "Personal Macro Workbook."

5. Click 'OK' to begin recording. Now, perform the tasks you want to automate, such as selecting cells, applying formats, and inserting formulas. Excel records all these actions.

6. Once done, return to the Developer tab and click 'Stop Recording'. Your macro is now stored and ready for use.

Utilizing Your Macro

To run your macro, you can either use the shortcut key you assigned earlier or navigate to Developer -> Macros, select your macro from the list, and click 'Run'. Watch as Excel replicates your actions precisely and consistently.

Editing a Recorded Macro

What if you need to make adjustments to your macro? The beauty of Excel is not just in performing tasks but also in its flexibility to adapt.

1. Go to Developer -> Macros, select your macro, and click 'Edit'. This opens the Visual Basic for Applications (VBA) editor, showing the code generated by your recording.

2. VBA might initially look intimidating, but with a few guidelines, you can start tweaking your macro. For example, if your macro includes a specific reference to a range of cells that might change next time you use it, you can edit those references to more generic ones.

3. If you recorded a mistake, simply locate that part of the code and modify or delete it. Remember, each line of recorded code corresponds to an action you performed.

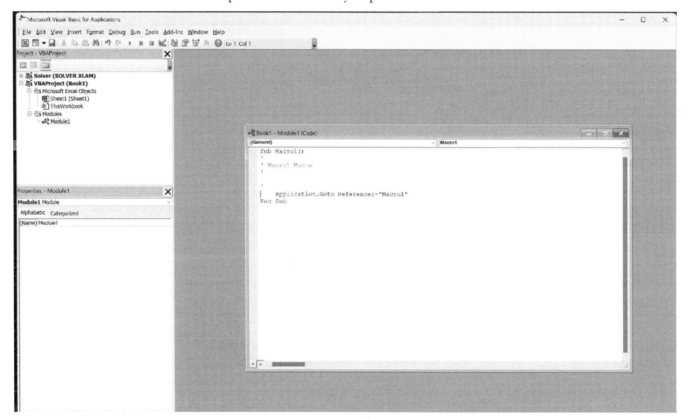

Practical Tips for Macro Efficiency

- Always test your macro in a safe environment before running it on critical data. An extra spreadsheet for testing can save you many headaches.

- Keep macros as short and specific as possible. This not only makes them easier to maintain but also minimizes the chances of errors.

- Document your macros. Adding comments in your VBA code by starting a line with an apostrophe can help you and others understand what each part of the macro does, making future edits easier.

Applying Macros to Real-World Scenarios

Consider a scenario where you receive weekly sales reports that need to be consolidated into a monthly report. By creating a macro that formats each weekly report identically and then another macro that consolidates these formatted reports into a single document, you significantly reduce the time spent manually performing these tasks.

Troubleshooting Common Macro Issues

If your macro doesn't work as intended, check for common issues like references to specific cells that may not exist in every sheet or operations that depend on certain conditions being met. The debugging tools in VBA are there to help you step through your macro one action at a time, allowing you to pinpoint and fix issues.

By mastering the basics of Excel macros, you unlock a level of efficiency that transforms how you handle data. This newfound skill not only enhances your productivity but also positions you as a competent and resourceful Excel user, ready to tackle complex challenges with confidence.

MACRO MODIFICATIONS WITH VISUAL BASIC FOR APPLICATIONS

Harnessing the full potential of Excel macros often involves more than just recording actions. For those who are ready to take their Excel skills further, diving into Macro Modifications with Visual Basic for Applications (VBA) opens up a universe of customization and efficiency. VBA is the programming language behind Excel macros, and understanding its fundamentals is key to transforming your standard macros into tailored tools that fit perfectly into your workflows.

Let's begin our journey into the deeper aspects of macro modification by first understanding how to access and navigate the VBA environment. Once you've recorded a macro, you can view and modify the underlying code by navigating to the Developer tab and clicking on 'Macros'. Choose the macro you wish to edit and click 'Edit'. This action launches the VBA editor, revealing the code that makes your macro tick.

VBA might look intimidating at first glance, but with some basic understanding, you can begin to tweak your macros with precision.

The editor window displays lines of code, each representing a specific action or instruction in your macro. Here's where clarity in your modifications counts. Suppose you recorded a macro that formats a report, but you now need to adjust it for reports that vary slightly in structure. By understanding and modifying the VBA code, you can make your macro more versatile.

A common scenario might involve modifying cell references in your macro. Initially, your macro might be coded to apply formatting to a specific range like "A1:A10". If you find that your reports occasionally contain more rows, you can edit this range directly in the VBA code or program the macro to dynamically adjust to the amount of data present.

Beyond simple edits, VBA allows for more complex modifications such as incorporating conditional statements. Imagine you want your macro to perform certain tasks only if specific conditions are met, like only tallying cells that contain numbers greater than zero. In VBA, you can use an 'If' statement to make this happen:

If Cell.Value > 0 Then ' Code to execute if the condition is true End If

Introducing loops is another powerful modification. Loops can instruct your macro to repeat a set of actions multiple times, which is invaluable for tasks such as processing data across multiple rows or columns. For example, a 'For' loop in VBA can be used to go through all rows in a dataset:

For Each Row in Range("A1:A100") ' Code to execute for each row Next Row

Understanding errors and debugging them is an essential skill when modifying macros. VBA provides debugging tools that allow you to step through your macro line by line, watch how data changes during its execution, and pinpoint where errors occur. Learning to use breakpoints and the Immediate Window can drastically reduce the time you spend troubleshooting.

In practice, let's consider a scenario where you need a macro to summarize data, but only if that data meets certain quality criteria. By modifying your macro to first check data quality, and then summarize only acceptable data, you ensure your reports are both accurate and reliable.

To further extend the functionality of your macros through VBA, you can also explore creating user-defined functions (UDFs), which are custom functions not built into Excel. These can be called directly from your worksheet and can act just like native Excel functions. This is particularly useful for performing specialized calculations custom-tailored to your specific needs.

Modifying macros in VBA emphasizes not just the automation of tasks but the intelligent automation of tasks tailored effectively to your operational requirements. By building a solid foundation in VBA, you can turn your macros into powerful tools that perform exactly as you need them to, saving you time and enhancing the reliability of your work.

Adjusting to handle Excel macros with VBA doesn't just enhance your spreadsheets — it transforms the way you manage information, making your data work smarter and harder for you. It's about making Excel not just a tool, but a trusted partner in your data analysis efforts.

With practice, patience, and a detailed focus on customization through VBA, your journey from macro recorder to macro innovator will not only be successful but also enjoyable.

CREATING CUSTOM MACRO-DRIVEN INTERFACE ELEMENTS

Excel is more than a powerhouse for data manipulation—it can transform into a highly interactive environment that custom-tailored to your specific workflows, thanks to custom macro-driven interface elements. When you delve into creating these custom elements, you're not just optimizing your tasks but also enhancing the entire user experience.

One of the most transformative ways to utilize macros in Excel is by integrating them into custom interface elements such as buttons, forms, and sliders. These elements not only make your spreadsheets more intuitive and accessible but also allow users of all skill levels to interact with your data without necessarily understanding the complexities underneath.

Integrating Macros with Form Controls

Imagine a scenario where you need to present a dataset for non-technical stakeholders who require the ability to adjust variables to see potential outcomes. By using form controls linked to macros, you can create a user-friendly dashboard that allows users to manipulate variables through sliders, check boxes, or option buttons. Each interaction triggers a macro that performs complex computations and updates the data displayed.

To create this dynamic setup, start by adding form controls from the Developer tab. You can find options under 'Insert' in the Controls group. Here's how you can integrate a simple form control with a macro:

1. Add a button from the Form Controls.

2. Right-click the button and select 'Assign Macro…'.

3. Choose the macro that you've previously recorded or written, which might be something like refreshData(). Now, whenever the button is clicked, it triggers the macro, executing pre-defined actions.

Creating an Interactive Dashboard

Using the example above, let's expand it into creating a complete interactive dashboard. Suppose you have a sales dataset and you want to see how changing certain parameters like discount rate or sales region affects the total sales.

1. Along with the button to refresh data, add sliders for discount rate and option buttons for selecting regions.

2. Link each control to a specific macro that calculates sales based on the selected parameters.

3. Enhance visibility by inserting a chart that dynamically updates as parameters change. Now you have a dashboard that's not only functional but also a powerful tool for data analysis.

Utilizing Userform in VBA

For more complex interactions, you can utilize Userforms in VBA, which are customizable dialog boxes. These are particularly useful for inputs that require specific formatting or multiple data fields. For instance, if you are managing an inventory and need a form where users can add new items, Userforms make it possible. Creating a Userform involves:

1. Opening the VBA editor from the Developer tab.
2. Inserting a Userform via Insert -> UserForm.
3. Adding controls like text boxes, labels, and buttons from the Toolbox into the Userform, setting properties like size, text, and color as per your needs.
4. Writing VBA code for each control to specify what happens when data is entered into the form or a button is pressed.

This setup takes your functional abilities a notch higher, making data entry and retrieval not only easier but also error-free, as you can set validation rules directly within the form.

Practical Tips for Enhancing Macro-Driven Interfaces

- Always keep the end-user in mind. Customize the interface to be intuitive and easy to navigate.
- Use labels and tooltips generously to guide users on how to use the interface elements.
- Test the interface thoroughly to ensure that macros trigger correctly and that all form controls are responsive.

Real-World Application Example

Consider a retail business that uses an Excel-based system for inventory management. By integrating a Userform that staff can fill out when adding new stock items, coupled with buttons to calculate restock levels or generate reorder reports, you significantly streamline the inventory process. This not only saves time but also reduces the risk of manual errors.

By developing these custom macro-driven interface elements, you push Excel from being just a data processing application to being an interactive, self-service tool for all users. Whether it's through simple form controls or complex Userforms, the integration of macros into Excel's interface not only enhances functionality but also empowers users to interact with data in ways that were previously out of reach. These capabilities enable users not just to work on data, but to experience it, leading to deeper insights and more impactful decisions.

VBA SCRIPTING FOR TASK AUTOMATION

Exploring the capabilities of VBA (Visual Basic for Applications) in Excel takes macro utilization from just recording repetitive tasks to creating fully automated custom solutions. VBA Scripting is a powerful tool integral to optimizing processes, enhancing productivity, and transforming the interaction dynamics with massive datasets. This enhanced automation capability makes VBA indispensable for advanced Excel users.

Understanding VBA and Its Environment

VBA in Excel is more than just a series of recorded steps; it's a programming environment that allows you to write and execute functions that interact directly with your workbook. To get started, access the VBA editor by pressing ALT + F11 from within Excel. This brings up a new window that might resemble a simplified version of other programming environments you've seen, complete with project explorer on the left and a code window.

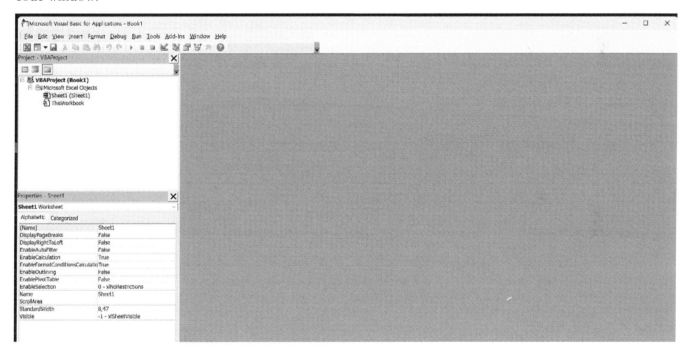

The First Script: Automating Repetitive Tasks

Think about a simple daily task, such as formatting new data entered into a spreadsheet at the end of the day. Typically, this might involve setting border styles, adjusting cell colors based on conditions, or summarizing data into another spreadsheet. With VBA, you can script these actions and automate them.

Start with creating a new Subroutine (often just called a "Sub" in VBA). A Sub is simply a block of code that performs actions. For example:

vba Sub FormatDailyReport() With Sheets("Daily Report") .Range("A1:D1").Font.Bold = True .Range("A1:D1").Borders(xlEdgeBottom).LineStyle = xlContinuous End With End Sub

This simple script sets the first row of the "Daily Report" sheet to have bold text and a bottom border. Once this script is run—either by tying it to a button or executing it directly within VBA—it performs the formatting instantly.

Expanding Functionality with Loops and Conditions

Once you've mastered simple tasks, VBA allows you to incorporate logical conditions and loops. Suppose you want to check through a column of data and highlight cells where the value is below a certain threshold:

vba Sub HighlightLowValues() Dim cell as Range For Each cell In Sheets("Sales Data").Range("B2:B100") If cell.Value < 50 Then cell.Interior.Color = RGB(255, 0, 0) ' Red background End If Next cell End Sub

This script checks each cell in the range B2 to B100 of the "Sales Data" sheet. If a cell's value is less than 50, it changes the cell's background color to red. Tasks like this show the true power of VBA, allowing for complex, conditional logic to be applied across large datasets quickly.

Integrating User Interaction

As VBA develops, you may need scripts that interact with the user, requesting inputs or providing choices. VBA can handle this through message boxes and input boxes:

vba Sub GetUserInput() Dim userResponse As Integer userResponse = MsgBox("Do you wish to continue? (Yes/No)", vbYesNo) If userResponse = vbYes Then MsgBox "User chose Yes." Else MsgBox "User chose No." End If End Sub

This script displays a message box asking if the user wishes to continue, with "Yes" and "No" buttons. Depending on the user's choice, another message box confirms the selection. This kind of interaction is instrumental when deploying scripts that require user decisions before proceeding.

Best Practices for VBA Scripting

- **Comment your code generously**. VBA scripts can become complex, and maintaining them without good comments can become nearly impossible.
- **Keep security in mind**. Ensure your scripts do not expose sensitive data inadvertently, especially when sharing macros or entire workbooks.
- **Debug systematically**. Utilize VBA's built-in debugging tools to step through your code, watch variable values, and handle errors effectively.

Real-World Application

Consider an inventory management system where new inventory data is entered daily. Using VBA, develop a script automating the creation of daily reports, checking inventory levels, and alerting via email if certain stock items are low. This level of automation not only reduces daily manual input but also helps prevent errors, making the inventory system more robust and responsive.

By using VBA in Excel, you transform from a passive data handler into a proactive data manager. Your ability to manipulate, analyze, and interact with information becomes significantly enhanced, turning complex tasks into automated processes that not only save time but also increase accuracy and efficiency in your work environment.

CHAPTER 13: VISUALIZING DATA THROUGH DASHBOARDS

Imagine walking into a boardroom, where on the giant screen, a dazzling dashboard displays real-time data, seamlessly integrating charts, tables, and slicers. Everyone in the room can instantly see the current business standings and make decisions based on the data visualized right in front of them. This is the power of using Excel to create dashboards, and in this chapter, we're going to unlock this power together.

Dashboards are vital tools in modern data analysis, providing a visual summary of complex data, which allows you to see trends, outliers, and patterns that might not be apparent in traditional reports. They are less about the raw data and more about the story that your data tells—whether it's the year-over-year growth in sales, the performance metrics of different departments, or tracking customer behavior.

Creating an effective dashboard is both an art and a science. It begins with identifying which data is most important to your audience. What do they need at their fingertips? How can they interact with the data to get the information they need? We'll start by structuring our data using PivotTables, which offer a dynamic way to rearrange and aggregate complex data simply and effectively.

Next, we will dive into selecting the right types of charts that correspond not just to the nature of your data, but to the questions your data seeks to answer. A well-chosen chart can illuminate trends and inspire actions that might get lost in a standard spreadsheet view. For instance, a clustered column chart can clearly demonstrate comparative values, such as sales performance across different regions, while line charts might be used to show changes over time, like monthly revenue growth.

Then, we'll incorporate slicers and timelines. These tools help in refining what data appears on your dashboard, making it interactive. Imagine being able to focus your dashboard on a particular product line or time period with just a simple click. This interactivity enhances the user experience, allowing for instant customization and deeper analysis.

By the end of this chapter, you'll be equipped not only to construct your own interactive dashboards but also to ensure that they provide clear, actionable insights tailored to the specific needs of your business or project. This ability will no doubt elevate your reputation as someone who not only understands their data but can also make it speak persuasively to others. Now, let's start this journey together and transform your data into a compelling, visual story.

CONSTRUCTING INTERACTIVE DASHBOARDS WITH PIVOT CHARTS

Imagine you are tasked to present a quarterly report at the upcoming board meeting. You could distribute a typical spreadsheet filled with figures or you could captivate your audience with a dynamic, interactive dashboard that not only represents your data clearly but also allows users to explore aspects relevant to them. This is where mastering the art of creating interactive dashboards with Pivot Charts comes into play.

Getting Started with Pivot Charts

Pivot Charts in Excel are powerful visual tools that help in transforming rows of data into meaningful visuals. They are inherently connected to PivotTables, providing a graphical representation of the summarized data, making them ideal for dashboards.

Step 1: Lay the Groundwork with a PivotTable

Your journey to a compelling Pivot Chart starts with a well-structured PivotTable. Let's say you are dealing with sales data. First, insert a PivotTable by selecting your data range and choosing Insert > PivotTable. Once created, decide on the layout. Drag fields to different areas (Filters, Columns, Rows, and Values) based on what you need. For our sales report, placing 'Product Category' in Rows and 'Revenue' in Values gives a good start.

Step 2: Create Your Pivot Chart

With your PivotTable ready, simply select any cell within it and go to Insert > PivotChart. Choose the chart type that best represents your data. If you're summarizing sales data across different product categories, a bar chart might be the most illustrative. Excel will insert a Pivot Chart linked to your PivotTable.

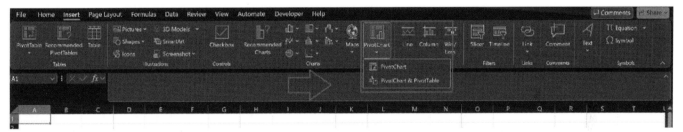

Customizing Your Pivot Chart

A generic chart may convey the basic data points, but customizing it can enhance its clarity and impact.

Adjusting Chart Elements

- **Titles and Labels**: Add clear titles to your chart and axes. For instance, your main title could be "2024 Q1 Sales by Product Category".
- **Data Labels**: These can be toggled on to display exact figures on the chart elements themselves, enhancing the informativeness at a glance.

Formatting for Clarity

Use color wisely. Highlight the most important data series in a contrasting color to draw attention. Utilize consistent color schemes that align with your company branding for a professional appearance.

Making It Interactive

The true power of Pivot Charts in dashboards lies in their ability to be interactive, allowing users to explore the data from different angles.

Slicers and Timelines

Add slicers by selecting your Pivot Chart and navigating to PivotTable Analyze > Insert Slicer. Choose the fields which will be most beneficial for deeper analysis, like 'Sales Region' or 'Sales Representative'. These slicers enable viewers to filter the data directly from the dashboard, narrowing down to what's most relevant to them.

Timelines work similarly but are geared towards date fields, allowing for swift filtering by time periods. This is especially useful in trend analysis over months, quarters, or years.

Drill-down Features

Excel's drill-down feature can be a game-changer. By double-clicking on a chart element, viewers can see the underlying data that makes up the figures. This feature must be set up to maintain the integrity and privacy of the sensitive or unnecessary data but can be invaluable in providing context right when it's needed.

Applying Real-World Scenarios

Now, picture using this interactive dashboard in different scenarios. For a sales manager, this tool can instantly show which products are underperforming. For the finance team, it translates broad numbers into digestible financial health indicators over different periods.

Consider a scenario where regional sales data is studied during a meeting. With a slicer set for regions, each manager can click on their respective region in the dashboard and instantly the chart updates to reflect just their data. It not only saves time but also adds a layer of engagement in meetings, making them more interactive and decision-focused.

Best Practices and Tips

- **Keep it simple**: Do not overload your dashboard with too many elements. Focus on what's most important.
- **Refresh your data**: Ensure your data source is always updated. A dashboard with outdated data loses credibility.
- **Test interactively**: Before presenting, click through all interactive elements to ensure they work seamlessly and the data updates as expected.

In summary, Pivot Charts enhance your ability to present complex data in an insightful, interactive, and visually appealing manner. By transforming your raw data into an engaging story, you empower your colleagues to make informed decisions quickly and confidently. With this tool, you don't just report data—you bring it to life.

DYNAMIC REPORTING WITH SLICERS AND TIMELINES

In the world of data management, understanding the story your data tells is as crucial as the data itself. With Excel's dynamic reporting features, such as slicers and timelines, you can transform static sheets into vibrant, interactive dashboards that allow your colleagues or clients to engage with the information like never before. This sub-chapter explores how to effectively utilize slicers and timelines to craft reports that are not only informative but also intuitive and adaptable to varying user needs.

Setting Up Slicers for Enhanced Interaction

Slicers are visual filters that allow viewers to segment data easily according to different criteria without ever needing to dive into complex filter menus. Imagine an Excel dashboard tracking sales performance across various regions. With slicers, a regional manager can simply click on their region in the slicer panel and the dashboard will instantly reflect data pertinent only to their area of concern.

Implementing Slicers

Start by setting up a PivotTable that summarizes the data you want to report. For example, if your dataset includes sales across different states for various products, create a PivotTable that aggregates sales by state and product category.

Once your PivotTable is ready, generating a slicer is straightforward: 1. Click anywhere inside your PivotTable. 2. Go to the PivotTable Analyze tab in the ribbon and select Insert Slicer. 3. Choose the fields for which you want to create slicers. For a sales report, you might choose 'State' and 'Product Category'. 4. Once created, you can position and format slicers to fit the layout of your dashboard.

Customizing Slicers for Clarity and Usability

- **Formatting**: Excel allows you to change the color, style, and size of slicers to match your dashboard's theme. It's beneficial to use distinct colors for different slicers to help users quickly identify the filter they need.
- **Arrangement**: Place slicers logically near the data they influence. Ensuring intuitive placement can significantly enhance the user experience.

Utilizing Timelines for Time-Based Data Filtering

Timelines are a specific type of slicer designed for filtering dates, which significantly enhances the functionality of dashboards that include time-series data. A financial dashboard, for instance, becomes much more powerful with a timeline allowing stakeholders to explore trends over different periods quickly.

Creating a Timeline

Building a timeline follows a procedure similar to that for slicers: 1. Ensure your data source includes properly formatted date fields. 2. Click on any date within your PivotTable. 3. Select Insert Timeline from the PivotTable Analyze tab. 4. Choose the date field for your timeline.

Timelines offer a user-friendly interface where you can select ranges simply by dragging across a time bar — a seamless method to shift views from monthly to quarterly data, for example.

Interactive Dashboard Design Considerations

When integrating slicers and timelines into your dashboards, here are some practical design tips to enhance functionality and user interaction:

- **Clear Labels and Instructions**: Always label slicers and timelines clearly. Include brief instructions or tooltips that guide new users on how to interact with the dashboard.
- **Responsive Layout**: Ensure that your dashboard elements rearrange gracefully when slicers or timelines are used. Overlapping elements or jumbled visuals can severely detract from usability.
- **Test User Interactions**: Before finalizing your dashboard, conduct user testing sessions. Observing real users interacting with the slicers and timelines can provide invaluable insights into further refinements.

Real-World Application and Benefits

Let's consider a real-world scenario: a retail company uses an Excel dashboard to track inventory and sales. By implementing slicers, the company's management can quickly isolate data for specific items, categories, or locations. Similarly, timelines help them review sales trends over various time frames — crucial for making informed stocking decisions.

For example, during a monthly meeting, a manager might use the timeline to show how sales have progressed through the quarter and then use slicers to drill down into specific weeks where unusual sales patterns appear. This ability to dynamically interact with the data leads to deeper insights and more productive discussions.

In summary, slicers and timelines are not just tools for data filtering — they are instruments for storytelling, allowing you to present a narrative that adapts to the inquiries and interests of the audience. By mastering these tools, you enhance not only the visual appeal of your dashboards but also their utility, leading to smarter, data-driven decision-making.

SYNTHESIZING CHARTS AND TABLES INTO DASHBOARDS

Excel dashboards are dynamic storytelling tools that visualize data in a way that is immediately understandable and engaging. Often, these dashboards combine charts and tables to summarize complex information, enabling quicker decision-making and more in-depth data analysis. When integrated thoughtfully, charts and tables can complement each other, providing both granular detail and big-picture insights. This sub-chapter guides you through synthesizing charts and tables into cohesive, impactful dashboards.

The Role of Charts in Dashboards

Charts are excellent for presenting trends, relationships, and patterns in data visually. By integrating charts such as bar graphs, line charts, and scatter plots into your dashboards, you can highlight significant aspects of the data that might not be immediately apparent from raw numbers alone.

Selecting the Right Charts

Choosing the appropriate type of chart is crucial. For instance, line charts are perfect for showing changes over time, making them ideal for sales trends or market analysis. Bar charts, on the other hand, are suitable for comparing quantities across different categories. Pie charts can be used to show proportions but use them sparingly as they can be difficult to interpret when there are many categories.

Customizing Charts

Ensure that your charts are not only informative but also aesthetically pleasing and aligned with the overall design of your dashboard: - Use consistent color schemes across all charts for a unified look. - Add chart titles, legends, and labels to enhance readability. - Adjust the axis scales so that the data presentation is clear and precise.

Integrating Tables for Detailed Data

While charts provide visual summaries, tables offer detailed numerical data necessary for a deeper understanding or specific inquiries. Tables in dashboards are particularly useful for displaying granular details, such as individual figures at a daily or transactional level.

Formatting Tables

A well-formatted table is easy to read and can gracefully fit into a dashboard without overwhelming other visual elements: - Highlight key figures using bold or color to draw attention. - Keep the table design clean and straightforward—avoid excessive borders or colors. - Use conditional formatting to bring out patterns or exceptions in the data, such as high or low values.

Combining Charts and Tables

When synthesizing charts and tables, placement and interaction are key. Each element should be positioned to guide the viewer naturally through the data.

Logical Layout

- Place high-level summary charts at the top or center of the dashboard as focal points.
- Situate detailed tables below or beside corresponding charts to provide an easy reference point for users seeking deeper insights.
- Ensure that the flow of information is logical and intuitive, leading from the general to the specific.

Interactive Elements

Enhance the dynamics of your dashboard by incorporating interactive elements: - Use slicers or filters that connect both charts and tables, allowing users to adjust what they see in real-time. - If using a software that supports it, set up drill-down capabilities in your charts that lead to more detailed data in your tables.

Practical Example

Consider a dashboard created for a retail management system, where the main screen shows a bar chart summarizing monthly sales across different regions. Directly below the chart, a table lists daily sales figures for selected regions. As regional managers choose their specific regions from a slicer, both the chart and the table update to reflect just the data relevant to their areas. This setup not only provides a quick summary but also allows for immediate access to detailed transactional data, all within the same cohesive visual space.

Best Practices

- **Consistency is Key**: Maintain consistent styles and formatting in both charts and tables to ensure the dashboard is cohesive.
- **Focus on Usability**: Keep user experience in mind. Overloading a dashboard with too much information can be overwhelming. Highlight the most important data and provide clear navigation.
- **Test and Iterate**: Gather feedback from actual users and be prepared to refine your dashboard. What works well in theory might need adjustments in real-world use.

Creating effective Excel dashboards is about more than just displaying data; it's about integrating various data visualizations into a coherent and interactive story that is easy to understand and act upon. With thoughtful design, appropriate chart and table integration, and attention to user interaction, your dashboards can become indispensable tools in your data analysis toolkit.

EFFECTIVE DATA DISPLAY TECHNIQUES

In a world brimming with data, effective presentation is the key to ensuring information isn't just delivered but is also understood and actionable. This sub-chapter addresses fundamental and advanced techniques for displaying data effectively in Excel dashboards. The goal is to tailor these dashboards not only to provide insights but also to engage the viewer, highlighting trends and critical points efficiently.

Understanding the Role of Visual Hierarchy

Visual hierarchy in data display is pivotal; it guides the viewer's eye to the most important pieces of information first. This hierarchical structuring is achieved through the strategic use of sizing, coloring, and placement of visual elements.

Size: Larger elements naturally draw more attention. Thus, the most crucial data, perhaps yearly revenue or total user engagement metrics, should be displayed in larger fonts or bolder charts.

Color: Utilize color to differentiate data sets or to highlight critical data points. However, use bright colors sparingly to avoid overwhelming viewers and diluting the impact of key data.

Placement: Position essential information in areas where eyes tend to go first—the top left of a dashboard is standard for cultures that read left-to-right.

Selecting the Right Charts

Choosing the appropriate chart types is crucial in data communication. The choice depends highly on the type and context of the data:

Line Charts: Ideal for displaying data trends over time. Use this when you want to show how data has changed on a continuum and where predictions might be necessary.

Bar Charts: Effective for comparing quantities across different categories. Vertical bar charts are useful for showing data when labels are lengthy.

Pie Charts: Best reserved for when you need to show parts of a whole, but these should be used sparingly, especially if there are more than five categories, as they can become difficult to interpret.

Balancing Detail and Clarity

An effective dashboard balances the fine line between being detailed and remaining clear. Overloading a dashboard with every possible metric can lead to confusion rather than clarity.

Aggregation and Summarization: Use summaries like averages, totals, or growth percentages to present a clear view of the data without oversimplification that could mislead the viewer.

Drill-Down Capabilities: Provide options for users to drill down into more detailed data if they choose. This capability allows users who need to explore more granular data to do so without cluttering the initial view for everyone else.

Interactive Elements for Enhanced User Experience

Interactivity can transform a static dashboard into an engaging tool: - **Slicers and Timelines**: Allow users to filter data dynamically based on their interests or needs. - **Hover-Over Effects**: Display additional information when hovering over a certain data point or element, which keeps your dashboard clean while still offering detailed data when needed. - **Dynamic Charts**: Charts that update as filters are applied make your dashboards responsive and relevant across different views.

Consistency in Design

Maintain a consistent design throughout your dashboard to aid in usability and interpretation: - **Fonts and Styles**: Use consistent fonts, sizes, and colors to ensure that your dashboard communicates in a uniform voice. - **Legends and Labels**: Clearly label all charts and tables, and use legends where necessary. This is not just good design—it's crucial for accessibility. - **Themes**: Stick to a color theme throughout the dashboard, ideally reflecting corporate branding or the purpose of the dataset.

Real-World Application: Sales Performance Dashboard

Consider a sales team using a dashboard to track performance across different regions and products. The dashboard uses a combination of bar charts for sales comparisons, line charts for trend analysis over time, and conditional formatting in tables to highlight regions that are underperforming or excelling.

A well-designed dashboard would allow the team to quickly ascertain which products are performing well in which regions, how sales trends are changing, and where to focus efforts for improvement—all through a clear, visual representation.

Refining Based on Feedback

Always solicit and apply feedback from actual dashboard users. Observing how they interact with the tool and the questions they ask can provide invaluable insights into what works and what may need to be adjusted.

Creating effective data displays in Excel is not merely about making data "pretty" but making it resonate with clarity and impact. Properly executed, these techniques not only showcase data but also tell its story, ensuring that important insights do not get lost in translation. This approach forms a bridge between data and decision-making, facilitating a dialogue that is both informed and intuitive.

CHAPTER 14: SOPHISTICATED DATA ANALYSIS METHODS

Welcome to the sophisticated world of data analysis with Excel. Having mastered the basics and grabbed hold of intermediate skills, you are now entering the terrain where Excel stops being merely a tool and becomes an integral partner in unraveling the complex threads of data.

In this chapter, we delve into methods that aren't just about handling data, but about analyzing it to unearth patterns, predict trends, and make data-driven decisions that were obscure before. We explore high-level functions and features that lift the veil on Excel's most dynamic capabilities.

We'll start with **Goal Seek** and **Scenario Manager**, tools that turn Excel into a powerful decision-making ally. Imagine you're at a crossroads making financial forecasts—with these tools, Excel helps you navigate potential futures easily. From adjusting a single value to observing outcomes across multiple scenarios, we'll guide you through using these features to refine your forecasts and enhance your decision accuracy.

Then we shift gears to **Solver**—a more potent tool that tackles complex optimization problems. Whether maximizing profits, minimizing costs, or managing logistics, Solver represents Excel's capability to provide solutions that are not immediately obvious, delivering outcomes that optimize specified parameters.

Next, we'll look at enhancing your exploratory data analysis with **Slicers** and **Timelines** for interactive filtering, making vast data sets digestible and more accessible. This isn't just about seeing the data but interacting with it in a way that reveals the underlying stories.

The journey through sophisticated data analysis isn't complete without diving into **Power Query**, a feature that automates the process of gathering and reshaping data from various sources, readying it for deeper analysis. Whether you're pulling information from databases, files, or the web, Power Query simplifies the collection and transformation processes, allowing you more time to focus on strategic analysis rather than data prep.

By the end of this chapter, you'll not only be equipped with advanced tools but also with the confidence to use these tools to push the boundaries of what you can achieve with Excel. From predictive analytics to resource optimization, your journey through Excel's advanced data analysis capabilities will transform you from a user to an analyst, ready to take on complex challenges with a few clicks.

Ready to dive in? Let's unleash the full potential of your data with Excel's sophisticated analysis methods.

APPLYING GOAL SEEK AND SCENARIO MANAGER FOR PREDICTIVE ANALYSIS

For those ready to make the leap from simple data entry to strategic decision-making, Excel offers tools like **Goal Seek** and **Scenario Manager**, designed to be not just solutions but gateways into the world of predictive analysis. These tools empower you to simulate different scenarios and predict outcomes, helping influence decisions before committing to real-life actions.

Understanding Goal Seek

Imagine you're planning to apply for a loan. You know how much money you need, but you're unsure what your monthly payments should be to pay off the loan within a desired time frame, or how changing the interest rate might affect these payments. This is where **Goal Seek** shines.

Goal Seek is Excel's way of performing what-if analysis through back-solving methodology. It adjusts a value in one cell to achieve a desired result in another cell. Here's how you can harness this feature:

1. **Set Up Your Formula**: Start with a basic formula in Excel. For instance, the calculation of loan repayments with a formula in C1 = A1*(1 + B1), where A1 holds the loan amount and B1 the interest rate.

2. **Launch Goal Seek**: Go to the Data tab and select What-If Analysis, then click on Goal Seek. This opens the Goal Seek dialogue box.

3. **Configure Goal Seek**:

   o **Set cell**: Enter the cell that contains the formula you want to adjust (in our example, C1).

   o **To value**: Input the desired outcome (e.g., the specific monthly payment you aim to achieve).

   o **By changing cell**: Specify the cell to adjust to reach the goal (for instance, changing the interest rate in B1 to see how it affects the monthly repayment).

4. **Execute and Analyze**: Click OK, and watch as Excel recalculates the input to reach the desired goal. This instant result shows whether your targets are realistic under current constraints.

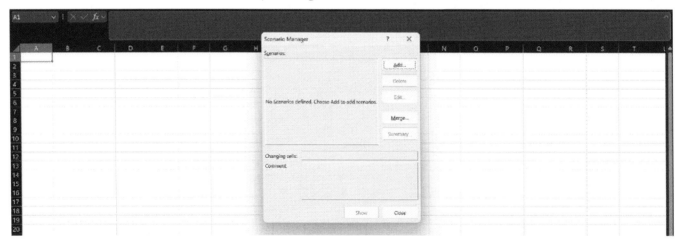

Exploring Scenario Manager

While Goal Seek adjusts a single parameter, **Scenario Manager** expands this by comparing the impacts of varying multiple parameters simultaneously. This feature is invaluable for strategic planning, where multiple factors affect the outcome.

Consider a small business assessing the financial forecasts under different market conditions. You might need to alter the price point, cost of goods sold, and marketing budget to understand different fiscal results based on varying market scenarios.

1. **Set Up Base Data**: Enter all relevant data points into a worksheet. Each variable (price, cost, budget) should be in a separate cell.

2. **Access Scenario Manager**: Navigate to What-If Analysis in the Data tab and select Scenario Manager. Click Add to create a new scenario.

3. **Create Scenarios**:
   - **Name the scenario** (e.g., "Optimistic Market Conditions").
   - **Changing cells**: Select the cells that will change in this scenario.
   - **Values for changing cells**: Input the values reflective of this scenario (higher price, lower costs, increased budget).
   - Repeat the process to create different scenarios, such as "Pessimistic Market Conditions" or "Stable Market Conditions".

4. **Run and Compare Scenarios**: Once scenarios are set up, click Show to view the outcomes of each or Summary to compare them side by side. This comparative view helps in understanding how changes in input variables might affect the overall performance of your business.

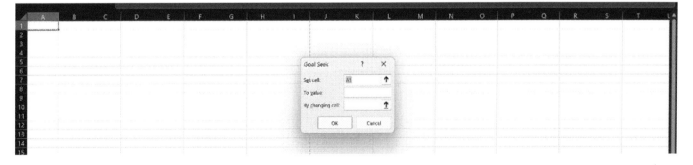

Practical Applications

Both tools are not only powerful but also versatile in various real-world contexts, from financial analysis and business forecasting to personal financial planning and even scientific experiments. Here's how you might apply them:

- **Business Forecasting**: Adjust production levels to meet financial targets or assess impact of changing market trends.

- **Loan Management**: Calculate how changes in interest rates or loan amount affect monthly payments.
- **Scientific Experiments**: Experiment with different input variables to observe changes in outcomes, thus helping in hypothesis testing.

Tip for Enhanced Usage

While both tools are powerful, using them in conjunction with **Data Tables** or **Pivot Tables** can further enhance your ability to analyze and visualize differences in scenarios or adjusted variables. This integrated approach not only centralizes your data analysis efforts but also streamlines them, making complex calculations and comparisons straightforward and transparent.

Leveraging **Goal Seek** and **Scenario Manager** effectively will turn your Excel spreadsheets from static tables of numbers into dynamic tools for decision-making. Remember, the goal is to not only predict outcomes but also to strategize around these predictions, crafting smarter, data-driven decisions in your professional and personal life.

OPTIMIZATION WITH SOLVER

When faced with complex decision-making scenarios where multiple variables and constraints are involved, Excel's Solver function emerges as a powerhouse, enabling you to pinpoint the optimal solution by adjusting the variables in your formula. This tool is invaluable for various high-level applications, from resource allocation to maximizing profitability and minimizing cost.

Imagine you are a business manager trying to determine the best combination of products to produce within cost and resource constraints or a dietitian designing a meal plan that meets nutritional standards at minimal expense. In all such cases, Solver helps by finding the best possible outcome that fits all given conditions.

Understanding Solver

Solver in Excel is essentially an optimization engine, capable of handling linear, nonlinear, and even integer programming problems. What sets Solver apart is its ability to manage multiple variables simultaneously, iterating through potential solutions until it finds the one that best meets your specified objective, while adhering to the constraints you've set.

Setting Up Solver

The first step in using Solver is defining the problem in Excel. Any optimization problem includes three main components you need to identify: 1. **Objective Cell**: This is what you want to optimize, such as profit, cost, or any other measurable outcome derived from a formula in Excel. 2. **Variable Cells**: These are the cells that

Solver will adjust to optimize the objective cell. They represent decision variables, like quantities of different products to manufacture or amounts of ingredients in a diet plan. 3. **Constraints**: These limitations guide Solver's adjustments to the variable cells. Constraints can be anything like budget limits, resource maximums, or minimum sales targets.

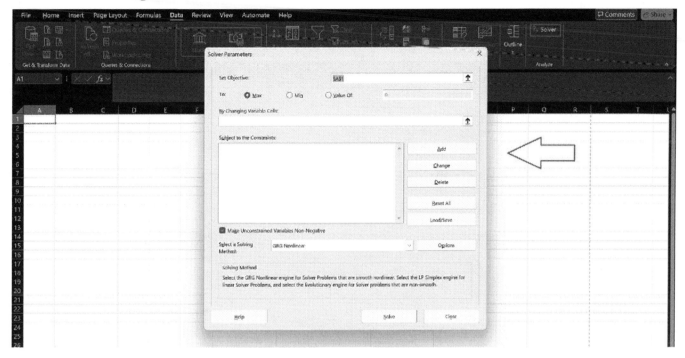

Implementing Solver

To activate Solver, you'll navigate to the 'Data' tab and click on 'Solver'. The Solver Parameters dialog box will then allow you to specify the objective cell, set the objective (maximize, minimize, or reach a specific value), and define the variable cells. Following this, you add constraints using the 'Add Constraint' dialog box, where you specify the constraint conditions for each variable.

For real-world interaction, consider you're optimizing a small-scale manufacturing process: - **Objective**: Maximize profit (calculated in cell F1). - **Variable Cells**: Number of each product to produce (cells A2 to A5). - **Constraints**: - Material usage limits (no more than 1000 kg of material, cell B1). - Budget constraint (not exceeding $10,000, cell C1). - Product demand constraints (each product needs to be produced in quantities of at least 100 units).

Running Solver and Interpreting Results

Once you set up and configure your model, click 'Solve' in the Solver dialog box. Solver then processes the data, iteratively adjusting the variable cells until it finds the optimal solution or determines that no solution exists within the specified constraints.

Upon completion, Solver presents a result dialog box. If an optimal solution is found, you can keep the solution, restore original values, or further explore the answer report, sensitivity report, and limits report, which provide detailed insights into how sensitive the solution is to changes in parameters, and what constraints are binding or not.

Practical Integration

The practical integration of Solver spans across industries. In finance, it helps in portfolio optimization to balance risk and return. In operations, it facilitates production scheduling to minimize costs while meeting customer demands. In human resources, it can optimize staff assignments considering qualifications and availability.

Tips for Effective Solver Use

1. **Start Simple**: Begin with fewer variables and constraints to understand how Solver behaves. Gradually add more complexity.

2. **Use Realistic Constraints**: Ensure that constraints reflect true limits and possibilities within your scenario.

3. **Validate Results**: Always cross-check Solver's outcomes with manual calculations or estimations to confirm plausibility.

Solver, with its robust capability to navigate through multiple, often conflicting constraints and find the best possible outcomes, is akin to having a high-powered computational colleague by your side. Harnessing this tool effectively means turning complex, intimidating decision matrices into clear, manageable paths.

By mastering these concepts and using Solver strategically, you transform from a passive data reporter into a proactive data strategist, making decisions that are not just good, but optimal.

ENHANCED DATA EXPLORATION WITH SLICERS AND TIMELINES

In the realm of advanced Excel uses, mastering the art of data exploration can drastically enhance your ability to make informed decisions. Excel's features like Slicers and Timelines are designed to refine this process, offering dynamic ways to interact and delve deeper into your data without getting lost in complexity.

Slicers and **Timelines** are tools specifically designed for pivot tables, pivot charts, and regular tables, helping you filter through large sets of data in a visual manner. They act as dashboards that simplify access to specific segments of data, allowing you to "slice" through data layers and analyze information from various perspectives quickly.

Understanding Slicers

A slicer is a graphical tool that allows you to simplify the filtering process in Excel tables, pivot tables, or pivot charts. Unlike traditional filtering techniques, which require you to dive into dropdown menus and check or uncheck boxes, slicers present a button that you can simply click to filter data based on that item.

Here's how you apply a slicer: 1. **Insert a Slicer**: Click on your pivot table or any range of cells in a standard table. Navigate to the Insert tab and select Slicer. Choose the field(s) you'd like to use as filters. Excel will then generate a clickable button interface for each unique item in the selected field.

2. **Use a Slicer**: Click on one or more buttons in the slicer to filter your table or pivot report based on those items. You can select multiple items by holding down the Ctrl key and clicking on additional slicer buttons.

3. **Format and Customize**: You can format slicers to match the theme of your reports – change colors, adjust button sizes, and even control the visibility of items with no data.

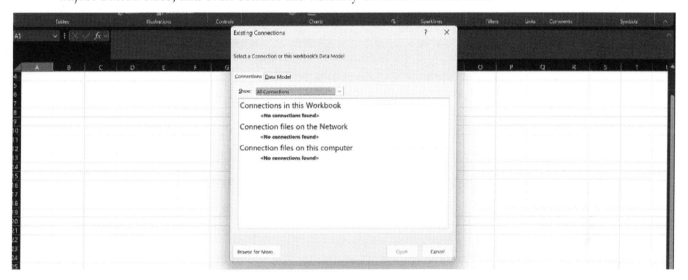

Exploring with Timelines

Timelines are particularly effective when working with data marked by dates. Like slicers, they provide a more intuitive and quicker way to drill down into periods of a time series directly from a pivot table.

Setting up a Timeline involves: 1. **Insert a Timeline**: With your pivot table active, go to the Insert tab and choose Timeline. This will prompt you to select the date field you want to use. Upon choosing the field, Excel places a timeline control into your worksheet.

2. **Using a Timeline**: Click and drag across the timeline bar to select the period that interests you. The pivot table or chart updates instantly to reflect data from the selected time period. You also select specific years, quarters, months, or days based on your need.

3. **Customization**: Timelines can be formatted for better integration with your document's design, adjusting colors, labels, and the time levels displayed.

Practical Applications

Imagine you are a sales manager analyzing quarterly sales data. By applying slicers, you can quickly isolate data for specific products, regions, or sales reps. A timeline, on the other hand, could help you focus on performance fluctuations through different seasons or compare the same quarters in sequential years.

Using these tools in conjunction not only accelerates the investigation of what's driving changes in your key metrics but also makes reporting these findings to stakeholders both faster and more impactful.

Advanced Tips for Using Slicers and Timelines

- **Connecting Multiple Tables**: You can connect a single slicer or timeline to multiple tables and pivot charts, ensuring they all respond simultaneously to your interface actions. This is ideal for dashboards that need to show different data aspects in coordination.

- **Layering Slicers**: You can layer multiple slicers related to different data fields. This method helps in narrowing down to very specific datasets, enabling detailed analysis without altering the worksheet structure or undergoing complex filtering processes.

Effective data exploration is about turning data into an insightful narrative. Slicers and Timelines don't just filter data; they transform how you interact with your data, promoting a deeper understanding through dynamic, visual representation. These tools are about bringing your data to life, making abstract numbers tell tangible stories that are crucial for making informed business decisions. With Slicers and Timelines, your journey through data becomes a dialogue, where every click unravels more insights, enabling you to navigate through the complexities of data with ease and confidence.

POWER QUERY FOR ADVANCED REPORTING

In the increasingly data-driven landscape of the modern business world, the ability to manage vast amounts of information efficiently is not just an advantage—it's a necessity. Enter Excel's Power Query, a powerful tool designed to transform, clean, and consolidate data in ways that traditionally would have required extensive programming skills. With its advanced data manipulation capabilities, Power Query has revolutionized the process of preparing intricate reports, making it easier and faster to derive actionable insights from raw data.

Exploring the Capabilities of Power Query

Power Query is an Excel add-in that allows you to discover, connect to, and import data from various sources. Whether the data comes from a local file, a database, web pages, or cloud services, Power Query provides a robust platform to retrieve and refine the information before it's even brought into your Excel workbook.

The real strength of Power Query lies in its ability to automate data transformation processes. This means once you set up a query to extract and transform data according to your specifications, the process can easily be repeated with fresh data, ensuring reports are up-to-date with minimal effort.

Setting Up Power Query

To get started with Power Query, follow these steps: 1. **Access Power Query:** Go to the Data tab on your Excel ribbon and select Get Data. Here, you'll find options to initiate new queries or load data from existing queries.

2. **Connecting to Data Sources:** Choose where to pull your data from. Power Query allows you to connect to files, databases, online services, and more. After selecting a source, Power Query will open an editor where you can view and transform the data.

3. **Editing and Transforming Data:** Once in the Power Query Editor, a plethora of options are available to modify your data. You can filter rows, transform formats, merge columns, and perform many other transformations. It uses a step-by-step model where each change you make to the data adds a new step in the query, which can be modified or deleted as needed.

Applying Advanced Transformations

One of the more advanced features of Power Query is the ability to merge and append queries. This is particularly useful when dealing with data split across multiple files or databases but needs to be reported together.

- **Merging Queries:** Suppose you have sales data in one table and customer information in another. Power Query can merge these tables by a common key, such as a customer ID. This consolidated view can then provide a deeper analysis of sales performance segmented by various customer demographics.

- **Appending Queries:** If you have similar data spread across different time periods, say monthly sales reports, Power Query can append these into a single table, making sequential analysis and year-over-year comparisons straightforward.

Refreshing Queries

One of the key benefits of Power Query is that after you load data into Excel, the query that brought it there remains connected to its source. This means you can refresh the data whenever the source is updated. This refreshed import can be set to happen automatically at scheduled intervals or done manually, ensuring your reports are always based on the latest available data.

Creating Reports

After transforming the data in Power Query, it can be loaded into an Excel workbook as a table or even directly into a Pivot Table. This immediate integration with Excel's reporting features allows seamless transition from data preparation to insightful analysis and reporting.

Optimizing Queries for Efficiency

Power Query performs a lot of data processing, and as such, efficiency in how you construct your queries can have significant impacts on performance: - **Filter Early, Filter Often:** Apply filters as early as possible in your queries to reduce the volume of data being processed in subsequent steps. - **Limit Columns:** Only load the columns you need for your analysis to avoid unnecessary data processing.

Challenges and Considerations

While Power Query is powerful, it's also complex. Here are quick tips to navigate some common challenges: - **Anticipate Data Changes:** Ensure your queries are robust enough to handle changes in the data structure from your sources, like additional columns or changes in data types. - **Debugging Issues:** Use the step-by-step transformation history in Power Query to debug issues by retracing and adjusting transformation steps.

Power Query is an indispensable tool for anyone who regularly works with varied and extensive datasets, providing capabilities that streamline the often-tedious aspects of data management. By automating data preparation tasks, Power Query not only enables more efficient data analysis workflows but also allows users to spend more time focusing on strategic data exploration and less time wrangling data. Embrace this tool within your Excel arsenal, and you transform your raw data into refined insights with unprecedented ease and speed.

CHAPTER 15: EXCEL EXTENSIONS AND INTEGRATION

As you delve deeper into your journey of mastering Excel, you've likely encountered moments where the foundational tools, while powerful, started to feel limiting in scope. This realization often comes as you begin manipulating larger datasets, integrating data from diverse sources, or needing more refined analytical capabilities. Chapter 15, dedicated to "Excel Extensions and Integration," is your gateway to transforming Excel from a solitary spreadsheet tool into a robust data manipulation powerhouse.

Imagine a scenario where you're not merely working on data but interacting with it in a dynamic and evolving environment. Here, Excel is not just an application but an integral part of a larger ecosystem that encompasses advanced data modeling, real-time analytical capabilities, and seamless integration with powerful tools such as Power BI. This chapter primarily focuses on introducing you to Power Pivot and Power BI—two of Excel's most formidable allies in data analysis and business intelligence.

For instance, with Power Pivot, you can manage immense datasets with a sophistication normally reserved for specialized software. It's like turning your Excel into a high-caliber data engine capable of sophisticated calculations and relationships that traditional pivot tables could never handle. The use of real-world examples here, such as consolidating financial data from different subsidiaries without having to leave Excel, will help cement your understanding of these complex concepts in a practical setting.

Furthermore, the integration with Power BI opens a new vista for Excel users. Think of Power BI as a storytelling medium where your data narrates the business scenario through interactive dashboards and rich visualizations, accessible across devices and empowering decision-makers with insights at their fingertips.

This chapter not only walks you through step-by-step processes to leverage these advanced tools but also intersperses expert tips to sidestep common pitfalls and enhance performance. For example, when setting up a Power Pivot model, you'll learn why setting correct data types is essential — a seemingly minor oversight that can significantly impact performance.

By the end of this chapter, your relationship with Excel will have evolved from basic data entry and manipulation to strategic data management and decision support, marking a pivotal point in your journey from novice to Excel maestro. This progression is aimed not just at enhancing your technical skills but at transforming the way you view and utilize data in real-world scenarios.

EXPLORING ADVANCED DATA MODELING WITH POWER PIVOT

In the world of Excel, where everyday functions like sorting, filtering, and basic formulas become second nature, there exists a frontier teeming with complex data challenges. As we explore the power of Excel as more than just a spreadsheet program, we step into the realm of Power Pivot—a tool designed specifically to enhance your data modeling capabilities.

This section will guide you through the art and mastery of advanced data modeling using Power Pivot, a crucial tool for those who need to manage large datasets more efficiently than standard Excel capabilities allow.

Power Pivot, when first encountered, may seem daunting. However, let's approach it with the story of Sarah, a data analyst in a mid-size retail company, tasked with managing sales data from over 100 stores nationwide. Sarah's challenge is not uncommon: the data is voluminous, filled with millions of rows that document everything from items sold per transaction to the time and date of purchases. Traditional Excel techniques struggled to handle such a vast array of data, but with Power Pivot, Sarah managed to transform her workflow by creating comprehensive data models.

Getting Started with Power Pivot

Your first step in Power Pivot is integrating it into your Excel environment. This process begins in the Excel Options menu, where you add Power Pivot by selecting it as an add-in. This action unlocks a new tab on your Excel ribbon, dedicating tools specifically designed for data modeling.

Creating Your First Data Model

Imagine importing multiple tables of data, such as sales, products, and store information. In Power Pivot, you can import data from various sources, including databases, feeds, and other Excel files, without overloading the worksheet. Connecting these tables is where Power Pivot's magic unfolds. You establish relationships between these tables, much like setting up a database. This linkage allows you to perform analysis across a spectrum of data without repetitive rows and the confusion multiple tables can typically introduce if just used in Excel.

Adding Calculations and Measures

Here is where Power Pivot starts to outshine basic Excel functionalities. You create measures using DAX (Data Analysis Expressions)—a formula language specifically for handling data. For example, if Sarah wanted to calculate the total sales across all stores, she could write a DAX formula to sum the 'Sales' column across her consolidated tables. These measures are dynamic, recalculating as your data refreshes and evolves.

Using Advanced Time Intelligence Functions

Power Pivot excels in analyzing data over time. Functions like TOTALYTD (Total Year-To-Date) or SAMEPERIODLASTYEAR offer profound insights for historical comparisons and trend analysations. Suppose Sarah wants to measure this year's sales performance against the last year's. Using these functions, she can quickly model this analysis, revealing trends and patterns critical for business strategy.

Building PivotTables and PivotCharts from Power Pivot Models

One of the paramount strengths of Power Pivot is its seamless integration with PivotTables and PivotCharts. Using the data model you've created, you can build PivotTables that draw on complex calculations and multiple data sources. The ability to drag and drop fields into a PivotTable supports intricate display setups, which is incredibly beneficial when dealing with multi-dimensional data.

Optimizing Data Models

As your data models grow more complex, optimization becomes crucial. One tip is managing the relationships wisely—too many unnecessary connections can slow down processes. Another tip is using 'Calculated Columns' judiciously. While they are powerful, they can also consume considerable memory and processing power if not used appropriately.

Practical Applications and Real-World Influence

Returning to Sarah's scenario, her use of Power Pivot has not only enhanced her ability to report on current data but has also significantly affected her company's strategic operations. Armed with rich, timely insights into sales trends, product performance across regions, and inventory needs, her company can make informed, data-driven decisions swiftly.

By following this guide through Power Pivot, you embark on a path that telescopes out from traditional Excel use, into a broader, more powerful way to manipulate and analyze data. Whether it's managing large datasets, performing complex calculations, or generating sophisticated reports, Power Pivot introduces an elevated level of proficiency to your Excel expertise.

As we close this section, remember that mastering Power Pivot is not just about handling data more effectively; it's about turning data into a strategic asset that can offer competitive edges and operational efficiencies. So, move forward with the confidence that you're well-equipped to tackle the challenges of data-heavy environments with finesse and strategic insight.

DEEP DATA ANALYSIS INTEGRATION WITH POWER BI

Navigating through the vast capabilities of Excel often leads to the discovery of its synergistic relationship with other powerful tools, particularly Power BI. In this part of our journey, we will explore how integrating deep data analysis from Excel into Power BI can elevate your data processing and visualization capabilities to an entirely new level. This advanced trajectory not only enhances your analytical skills but also prepares you to handle complex data scenarios with agility and insight.

Let us consider the story of Mike, a marketing analyst whose task is to understand consumer behavior and preferences spanning multiple product lines over several years. Excel, while robust, couldn't provide the dynamic visualization and live data integration necessary for real-time decision-making. This is where Power BI comes into play, offering a platform where Excel's data analysis is complemented by advanced visualization and data sharing capabilities

Integrating Excel with Power BI

The integration process begins by ensuring your data in Excel is clean and well-organized, which includes structured tables and clearly defined headers. Once your dataset is prepared, importing it into Power BI is quite straightforward. You can upload Excel files directly into Power BI Desktop, where tables and fields automatically pop up in your Power BI dashboard.

Creating Reports and Dashboards

Once your Excel data is imported into Power BI, the next step is to transform this data into interactive reports and dashboards. Power BI allows you to drag and drop fields to create visuals, much like PivotTables in Excel, but with a broader array of chart types and customization options. For example, Mike can quickly generate a scatter plot to analyze consumer trends or a heat map to visualize sales density across different regions.

DAX in Power BI

Furthering our exploration into data analysis, Power BI uses the same DAX (Data Analysis Expressions) language used in Power Pivot. This consistency means that formulas and measures you've created in Excel can be used directly in Power BI. Mike uses DAX to calculate year-over-year growth directly within his Power BI reports, ensuring his analyses remain consistent and are based on reliable calculations.

Real-Time Data and Sharing

One of the standout features of Power BI over Excel is its ability to handle live data feeds. Imagine Mike's dashboard updating in real time as sales data streams in during a product launch. This capability allows for immediate response and strategy adjustment, a critical advantage in fast-paced market environments. Moreover, Power BI dashboards can be shared across teams and stakeholders easily, providing a collaborative platform for data-driven decision making.

From Analysis to Action

Transitioning from analyzing data in Excel to performing deep data analysis in Power BI changes the narrative from static tables to interactive storytelling with data. For instance, Mike not only presents annual sales data but also incorporates market forecasts and interactive elements that allow executives to simulate various business scenarios directly from the dashboard.

This dynamic approach does not just visualize data but makes it an integral part of strategic conversations, where insights draw directly from the latest data. Power BI also offers the ability to publish reports and dashboards to the Power BI service, enabling access from anywhere, across devices, ensuring that stakeholders always have the most current insights at their fingertips.

Optimizing Performance in Power BI

As with any robust tool, there's a need for performance tuning, especially as your datasets grow. Optimizing data models in Power BI involves managing your data queries and understanding the refresh rates of your datasets. Practical tips include reducing data granularity where detailed data is unnecessary and managing your DAX queries to avoid overly complex calculations that can slow down performance.

Bridging Excel and Power BI into a Cohesive Unit

Ultimately, the goal is not to replace Excel with Power BI but to use them in harmony to enhance your data analysis capabilities. For Mike, Excel is still vital for detailed data manipulation and initial analysis phases. In contrast, Power BI provides the platform for bringing this analysis to life, through visualization and interactive reporting, making it a powerful extension of his Excel expertise.

By following these steps, you transform not just your approach to data but also elevate your analytical capabilities to incorporate broader business intelligence functions. This advanced integration not only enhances your competitive edge in the workplace but also bolsters your ability to influence strategic decisions based on comprehensive data analysis, epitomizing the true power of data in driving business success.

EMPLOYING SPECIALIZED THIRD-PARTY ADD-INS

In the expansive universe of Excel, where built-in capabilities stretch far and wide, there remains a landscape of custom solutions and enhancements contributed by third-party developers. These contributions come in the form of specialized add-ins, designed to extend and enrich your Excel experience, specifically tailored for tasks that may require highly specialized functionalities not available through standard Excel features.

Picture this: Linda, a financial analyst, often finds herself struggling with the intricacies of financial modeling and risk analysis.

While Excel is inherently powerful, she needs tools that specifically cater to the sophisticated financial calculations and simulations her job demands. This is where third-party add-ins play a crucial role, as they fill the gaps left by Excel's native functions.

Understanding Third-Party Add-Ins

Third-party add-ins are essentially software plugins developed to integrate seamlessly with Excel, providing additional features and utilities. These can range from simple functionality enhancements, like custom chart types, to more complex data analysis tools tailored for specific industries such as finance, statistics, or engineering.

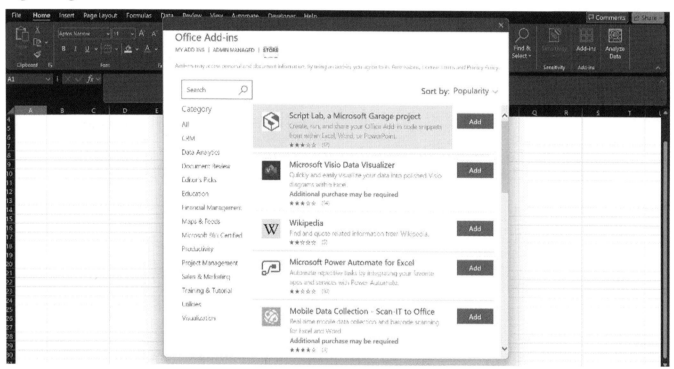

Selecting the Right Add-Ins

Choosing the right add-in depends largely on your specific needs. Linda, for example, opts for a well-known financial modeling add-in that not only accelerates her regular tasks but also introduces new methods that are endorsed by industry standards. When selecting an add-in, it is crucial to consider the reliability of the source, user reviews, and compatibility with your current version of Excel.

Installation and Security

Installing an add-in should be approached with caution. Always ensure that the source of the add-in is trustworthy, as poor-quality add-ins can pose security risks or affect the stability of your Excel setup. Most reliable third-party add-ins will come with an installer package that handles the setup process, and often, they'll provide an encrypted connection for registration and data handling, ensuring that your information remains secure.

Integration into Workflows

Once you've installed your chosen add-in, integrating it into your Excel workflow is usually straightforward. Most add-ins will add new tabs or groups to your Excel ribbon, giving you quick access to their features. Here, practicality comes into play – it's about streamlining tasks without overcomplicating your toolset. For Linda, the financial add-in she uses integrates naturally into her spreadsheets, adding new formulae directly into her Excel formula tab, making them as accessible as Excel's native functions.

Training and Utilization

Effective use of third-party add-ins often requires some learning and adjustment. Many add-in providers offer comprehensive tutorials and support forums. Engaging with these resources can significantly shorten the learning curve and help in leveraging the full potential of the add-in.

Real-World Impact

Let's consider how a real-world scenario is transformed by the application of a specialized third-party add-in. Linda, tasked with evaluating potential investment opportunities, uses her financial add-in to perform complex risk analyses. The add-in allows her to model various financial scenarios quickly, integrating real-time data feeds that keep her models up to date and relevant. This capability not only saves her hours of manual work but also increases the accuracy of her forecasts, providing her team with reliable data on which to base their decisions.

Maintenance and Updates

Maintaining the effectiveness of your add-ins involves keeping them updated with the latest software versions and ensuring compatibility with any new Excel updates. Most premium add-ins will provide automatic updates, but it's always good practice to check for updates periodically, especially after major Excel updates.

Networking and Community

Many third-party add-in users find great value in participating in user communities. These platforms allow users to share tips, discuss best practices, and provide feedback on the add-ins. Engaging with these communities can enhance your understanding and utilization of the add-in, often leading to better, more efficient use of Excel.

Evaluating Performance

Finally, regularly evaluate the impact of any add-ins on your Excel performance. While these tools are designed to enhance functionality, they can sometimes slow down your processes if not properly optimized or if they conflict with other add-ins or scripts.

By integrating specialized third-party add-ins into her Excel environment, Linda effectively enhances her analytical capabilities, moving beyond the conventional boundaries of Excel. This allows her not only to perform her job more efficiently but also to drive more nuanced insight and value from her data analyses, thereby affirming the power and versatility of Excel as augmented by third-party solutions. As you consider third-party add-ins, reflect on how they can complement your work in Excel, transforming your data analysis and broadening your capabilities within your professional sphere.

EXPANDING EXCEL FUNCTIONALITY WITH CUSTOM TOOLS

In the realm of Excel, where the built-in functionality is vast and expansive, there comes a point in every advanced user's journey where specific tasks or repetitive actions necessitate a more personalized toolset. This is where the creation of custom tools and the expansion of Excel's inherent capabilities become crucial. It places powerful and tailored utilities at your fingertips, ensuring that your unique data management and analysis requirements are met with precision.

Imagine you are Claire, a project manager overseeing large construction projects. The analysis encompasses everything from budget tracking and timeline forecasting to resource allocation. While Excel's standard features handle these tasks to some degree, the complexity and scale of Claire's projects call for a suite of custom tools that can automate repetitive tasks, integrate unique formulas, and create reports that cater specifically to her project's stakeholders.

The Role of Custom Tools

Custom tools in Excel are often developed using Visual Basic for Applications (VBA), a powerful programming environment built into Microsoft Excel. VBA allows for the creation of user-defined functions, automation scripts, and complex algorithms that can significantly reduce the time spent on routine data processing tasks.

Starting with VBA

Introducing VBA into your Excel skill set starts with learning the basics of the VBA editor, understanding how to write simple macros, and progressively tackling more complex scripting. For example, Claire could start by automating the task of compiling weekly financial summaries from various project databases.

Building User-Defined Functions

User-defined functions (UDFs) are one of the primary methods of expanding Excel's functionality. These are functions that you create in VBA to perform tasks that go beyond what built-in Excel functions can achieve.

For Claire, a custom UDF might calculate the expected costs of a project based on variable inputs like labor rates and material costs, something no standard Excel function offers directly.

Automating Repetitive Tasks

Automation is another critical area where custom tools can transform efficiency. By creating macros, you can automate tasks such as data entry, formatting, or even complex series of calculations. For instance, Claire uses a macro to automatically update her project timeline based on real-time data inputs from her on-site management teams.

Developing Custom Forms and Interfaces

For data entry and retrieval, custom forms can be designed to make the process more intuitive and error-free. These forms can be set up to guide users through the data entry process, ensuring that all necessary data points are correctly captured and formatted. Claire, for example, might design a form for site managers to enter daily resource usage, which directly feeds into her central project model.

Interactive Dashboards and Reporting Tools

Beyond processing and entering data, custom tools can also enhance the way data is presented and interacted with. Using VBA, you can create dynamic dashboards that allow users to filter, sort, and analyze data in real-time. Claire could develop a dashboard that lets her quickly assess the status of various aspects of her project, from budget adherence to timeline projections.

Real-World Application

Consider the impact of these custom tools in Claire's role. With her customized Excel dashboard, she can instantly view critical project metrics, update project stakeholders with visual, data-driven reports, and make informed decisions quickly. This capability not only enhances her efficiency but also improves the accuracy and reliability of her project management efforts.

Maintaining and Sharing Custom Tools

Maintenance is crucial to ensure that custom tools continue to function correctly as Excel updates or as new data structures are introduced. Regular reviews and updates of the VBA code and user interfaces can help mitigate any potential issues. Additionally, custom tools can be packaged and shared with colleagues who may benefit from similar functionalities in their work, further extending the value of your creations.

Evaluating the Efficiency of Custom Tools

Finally, it's important to continuously evaluate the effectiveness of any custom tools you develop. This involves testing for performance issues, gathering user feedback, and making iterative improvements. For Claire, receiving input from her team on the ground allows her to refine the tools to better meet the specific needs of each project phase.

By embracing the power of customization in Excel, you not only cater to your unique professional needs but also unlock new potentials in data management and analysis. Whether it's through automating mundane tasks, creating specialized functions, or developing interactive dashboards, the ability to expand Excel's functionality with custom tools is a pivotal advancement in any Excel user's career, embodying a shift from mere proficiency to true mastery.

CONCLUSION

As we draw near the end of our journey through the rich and multifaceted world of Excel, it's imperative to pause and reflect on the insights and skills you have gleaned from each chapter of this comprehensive guide. From mastering the basic functions in the early sections to dynamically utilizing complex formulas and creating macro-driven data analyses in the later chapters, your expedition through Excel has been both deep and wide-ranging.

Now, the Conclusion of this book is not merely a sign-off; it's a critical cornerstone that aims to knit together all the diverse strands of knowledge and practice you've encountered. Here, we summarize the essential takeaways from each segment, ensuring that you not only recall but integrate these insights into your daily use of Excel. This synthesis is vital as it transforms isolated pieces of knowledge into a cohesive toolkit you can readily deploy in your personal and professional life.

Moreover, as you step beyond the final pages of this guide, the journey with Excel doesn't halt—you are stepping onto a platform for continued learning and mastery. We'll outline strategies to keep enhancing your proficiency, from engaging with online forums and communities to experimenting with new plugins and updates from Microsoft.

Remember, each function and formula learned, each error encountered and solved, has propelled you closer to becoming not just proficient but powerful in using Excel. Transitioning from initially navigating basic spreadsheets to manipulating complex data sets with ease marks a significant growth in your skill set. By interlacing practice with practical tips and real-world scenarios, we've ensured that each step was clear, manageable, and most importantly, applicable.

So, as we gear up to summarize and conclude, let's reaffirm the knowledge acquired, explore avenues for further growth, and celebrate the potent tool Excel has transformed into in your capable hands. Embrace this moment as both a culmination and a commencement—a launchpad into your future endeavors with Excel.

SUMMARIZING KEY INSIGHTS FROM EACH VOLUME

Reflecting on our journey through "Excel Made Easy", we realize how each volume plays a unique role in shaping your capabilities. From foundation to advanced manipulation, the structured progression ensures that by the end of this guide, you're not just using Excel, but mastering it with confidence and finesse.

In our first volume, "Fundamentals of Excel Mastery," we laid the groundwork. Understanding the significance of Excel in modern workplaces, you learned how integral this tool is across sectors, helping everyone from business analysts to project managers streamline operations and enhance decision-making processes. The chapters within this volume introduced you to the core anatomy of Excel—starting from the user interface, moving through basic formula constructions and up to basic data management.

Remember how managing rows and columns seemed baffling at first? Now, resizing or moving these elements has become a task you can perform almost instinctively. This volume was designed to make you comfortable in the Excel environment, demystifying the grid layout and ensuring you could navigate through menus and toolbars with ease.

Transitioning into **"Developing Intermediate Excel Capabilities"** in our second volume, the aim was to build on the stable foundation laid previously. Your encounter with enhanced formatting tools, such as applying themes and styles, not only beautified your spreadsheets but made the data clearer and more digestible. Learning to manipulate data through features like Pivot Tables revealed Excel's capability to turn vast datasets into actionable insights. More significantly, introducing logical operations and data retrieval functions started shaping your problem-solving skills in data management. Every technique from freezing panes to using VLOOKUP was structured to boost your efficiency, preparing you to handle more complex tasks with increased confidence.

By the time we embarked on the third volume, **"Excel Proficiency for Advanced Users,"** you were ready to dive deep. The complexities of data management, such as using advanced data validation or protecting worksheets, were no longer daunting. You engaged with dynamic array formulas and macro automation—tools that aren't just about understanding Excel but mastering it to tailor its robust capabilities directly to your needs. We explored Dashboards and visual data presentation, transforming raw data into compelling, actionable visual reports.

Each volume was interspersed with practical examples tying Excel functions to real-world scenarios, making it evident how these tools apply directly to your everyday tasks and long-term projects. Whether it was organizing sales data, scheduling projects, or analyzing complex datasets for financial forecasts, the examples used were designed to resonate with your needs, reinforcing learning through relevance.

Moreover, practical tips dotted throughout these chapters ensured that you could sidestep common pitfalls and optimize your workflow. From keyboard shortcuts to customizing the Quick Access Toolbar, these nuggets of advice were about enhancing your speed, accuracy, and overall efficiency.

Stepping beyond the confines of this book's pages, these insights invite you to continue exploring Excel's possibilities. The tech landscape is ever-evolving, and with Excel continually updating, there will always be new features and tricks to discover. By laying a robust foundation and progressively building sophisticated skills, this guide has equipped you not just to adapt but to excel in future functionalities that Microsoft may introduce.

As we culminate this guide, it's important to recognize the transformation in your relationship with Excel. From initial hesitance to confident application, from basic operations to complex data analyses, your evolution is a testament to the power of structured learning. Each volume has not only been about imparting knowledge but also about inspiring you to challenge yourself, explore uncharted functionalities, and innovate in your use of Excel.

In embracing these capabilities, continually reflecting on the insights from each volume, and integrating them into your daily use, Excel becomes less of a software tool and more of a critical thinking partner in your professional narrative. Through this guide, our goal has always been to ensure that you stand not on the threshold but well within the realm of data mastery, equipped, empowered, and enthusiastic about the opportunities that proficient use of Excel unfurls in your career and beyond.

STRATEGIES FOR CONTINUED EXCEL PROFICIENCY ENHANCEMENT

As you turn the final pages of this guide, your journey into Excel mastery doesn't conclude—it evolves. Achieving proficiency in Excel is just the beginning: maintaining and enhancing your skills is crucial for staying relevant and adept in an environment where technological advancements and workplace demands continually evolve. Let's explore several strategies to ensure that your Excel skills not only remain sharp but also grow and adapt.

First, embrace the habit of regular practice. It's common to feel competent after initial successes; however, the depth of Excel lies in its frequent updates and added complexities. Set aside time weekly to experiment with new functions, or revisit complex formulas. This ongoing commitment transforms theoretical knowledge into practical expertise and ensures that your skills do not stagnate.

Second, leverage the power of community learning. Digital forums, social media groups, and online courses offer a wealth of knowledge and provide a platform for exchanging ideas and solutions. Platforms like Microsoft's Tech Community or dedicated Excel forums are treasure troves where users from around the world pose challenges, solutions, and innovative uses of Excel that you may never encounter in your day-to-day tasks. Engaging with these communities can provide insights into creative applications of Excel functions and introduce you to advanced techniques.

Continued education through structured courses or certifications can also profoundly impact your proficiency. Providers like LinkedIn Learning, Coursera, or even Microsoft offer courses that range from basic to advanced levels. Certifications, such as Microsoft Office Specialist in Excel, validate your skills and can markedly enhance your professional credibility and marketability.

Exploring Excel's integration capabilities with other tools offers another valuable method for enhancement. Excel does not operate in isolation but as part of a broader ecosystem involving tools like Power BI, Access, and various data visualization software. Understanding these integrations and learning to harness them can significantly boost your analytical capabilities and efficiency.

Another practical tip is to set personal or workplace projects that force you to stretch your Excel muscles. Whether it's automating a monthly report, analyzing sales data more profoundly, or even managing personal finances, practical applications of your skills lead to deeper understanding and innovation. Each project will likely teach you something new or propel you to find a solution to an unexpected challenge.

Keep abreast of updates and new features. Microsoft regularly updates Excel, each version bringing additional features and sometimes a new set of challenges. By staying updated with software changes and exploring new features as they are released, you can ensure that your skills remain current and robust.

Moreover, teaching others can surprisingly enhance your command of Excel. Whether it's mentoring a junior colleague, conducting a training session, or simply helping a friend, teaching is a powerful method to deepen your understanding and spot areas that need strengthening.

Finally, maintain a curious mindset. Excel is as much a tool for creativity as it is for calculation. The more you delve into its capabilities, experimenting with different functions and the power of their combinations, the more adept you will become at turning data into actionable insights.

These strategies form a framework for not just maintaining but actively enhancing your proficiency in Excel. As you continue to explore this powerful tool, remember that every function learned, every error encountered, and every challenge overcome is a step toward profound mastery. Evolving your skills with Excel is more than a professional requirement; it is a continuous journey of growth and discovery that mirrors the dynamic nature of the data-driven world around us. As you incorporate these strategies, keep pushing the boundaries of what you can achieve with Excel, always remembering that with each new skill acquired, new possibilities unfold.

SUGGESTED FURTHER LEARNING RESOURCES

Embarking on this journey to master Excel has, no doubt, expanded your understanding and skills. Yet, the landscape of Excel learning is vast and continually evolving. To further your expertise, a multitude of resources await, ranging from online courses and books to dynamic forums and workshops. Each of these avenues offers unique opportunities for deepening your knowledge and refining your skills, ensuring that your Excel journey is both enriching and enduring.

Online Courses and Video Tutorials Dedicated online platforms such as LinkedIn Learning, Coursera, and Udemy offer a variety of structured courses. These courses cover everything from introductory Excel skills to advanced techniques in data analysis and macro programming. Video tutorials, especially those on YouTube, provide visual and practical guides that are particularly beneficial for complex functions and visual learning preferences. Channels like ExcelIsFun exude comprehensive lessons with real-time examples that mirror everyday tasks.

Books and E-Books While this guide serves as a foundational text, further reading can deepen your understanding. Books like "Excel Bible" by John Walkenbach or "Excel Power Pivot & Power Query for Dummies" by Michael Alexander extend into specific tools that enhance Excel's functionality. E-books available on platforms such as Amazon Kindle often provide updated and accessible resources that you can carry with you and read on-the-go.

Webinars and Workshops Participating in webinars and workshops offers a more interactive learning experience. Organizations such as the Microsoft Office Specialist program provide sessions with experts that also allow for Q&A, giving you the chance to address specific challenges you encounter. Additionally, local community colleges and adult education centers frequently host hands-on Excel workshops.

Forums and Online Communities Engage with communities such as MrExcel, Tech Community by Microsoft, or the subreddit r/excel. These forums are goldmines for specific advice, novel solutions, and innovative uses of Excel that you may not encounter in formal education settings. The community members range from new users to advanced programmers, providing a wide spectrum of insights and solutions.

Podcasts and Blogs For those who find community stories and updates inspirational, podcasts like the "Excel Guru" podcast can provide both tips and interviews with leading experts. Blogs managed by Excel authorities like Chandoo.org or the MyExcelOnline blog deliver regular posts that keep you updated with the latest trends, tips, and tricks.

Conferences and User Groups Annual conferences like the Data Insights Summit or local user group meetups offer networking opportunities with other Excel professionals. These gatherings can provide insights into industry standards and upcoming features, as well as a chance to share practical advice and learn from real-world experiences.

Microsoft Learning Pathways Microsoft itself offers an array of learning pathways and certifications. These resources are invaluable for ensuring your skills stay current with the latest software versions. Microsoft's certification, such as the Microsoft Office Specialist: Excel Associate, not only educates but also enhances your professional profile.

In the spirit of continuous improvement, it's beneficial to set personal learning goals and periodically review these resources. As Excel evolves, so should your skills and strategies for using it. Keeping a pulse on new tools, formulas, and integration capabilities through these resources will ensure your abilities are both current and proficient.

By incorporating these resources into your ongoing learning plan, you can assure that your Excel skills continue to grow, adjusting not only to your personal and professional needs but also to the wider developments within data management and analysis. Remember, every tool or function you master not only enhances your proficiency but also opens new avenues for creativity, efficiency, and insight in your work.

With these resources at your fingertips, you're equipped to continue enhancing your Excel skills long after you turn the final page of this guide. Continue to explore, experiment, and excel. The journey doesn't end; it evolves.

SCAN THE QR CODE BELOW TO DOWNLOAD OVER 200 TEMPLATES:

Made in the USA
Columbia, SC
31 December 2024

50929136R00096